The Crusades in the Modern World

T0373510

Engaging the Crusades is a series of volumes which offer windows into a newly emerging field of historical study: the memory and legacy of the crusades. Together these volumes examine the reasons behind the enduring resonance of the crusades and present the memory of crusading in the modern period as a productive, exciting and much needed area of investigation.

The Crusades in the Modern World examines a broad range of contemporary uses of the crusades demonstrating how perceptions of the crusades are deployed in causes and conflicts today, and exploring the ways in which those perceptions are constructed and received. The use of crusading rhetoric and imagery to frame and justify violence presents an important recurring theme throughout the book, invoked by a range of diverse actors from Islamist terrorists like al-Qaeda and ISIS, to politicians in the post 9/11 world, and from populist movements in Europe reviving 'Reconquista' rhetoric, to a Mexican drug cartel. The use of the crusades for building national and religious identity repeatedly asserts its importance in the present, whilst chapters on academic engagement with the crusades and on the ways in which Wikipedia articles on the crusades are created highlight the ongoing challenges of constructing knowledge about crusading.

The Crusades in the Modern World is ideal for scholars of the crusades and medievalism as well as for military historians and historians of memory.

Mike Horswell completed his PhD at Royal Holloway, University of London, and his book – *The Rise and Fall of British Crusader Medievalism, c.1825–1945* – was published in 2018. He has taught at Royal Holloway, King's College London, and the University of Oxford and is currently researching, teaching and writing on the memory and legacy of the crusades in the modern era, from historiography to popular culture.

Akil N. Awan is a Senior Lecturer in Modern History, Political Violence and Terrorism at Royal Holloway, University of London. He is Founder and Chair of the Political Science Association's Specialist Group on Political Violence & Terrorism. His books include *Radicalisation and Media: Terrorism and Connectivity in the New Media Ecology* and *Jihadism Transformed: al-Qaeda and Islamic State's Global Battle of Ideas.*

ENGAGING THE CRUSADES

THE MEMORY AND LEGACY OF THE CRUSADES

SERIES EDITORS
JONATHAN PHILLIPS AND MIKE HORSWELL

Engaging the Crusades
The Memory and Legacy of Crusading
Series Editors: Jonathan Phillips and Mike Horswell, Royal Holloway,
University of London, UK.

Engaging the Crusades is a series of volumes which offer initial windows into the ways in which the crusades have been used in the past
two centuries, demonstrating that the memory of the crusades is an
important and emerging subject. Together, these studies suggest that
the memory of the crusades, in the modern period, is a productive,
exciting and much needed area of investigation.

In this series:

Perceptions of the Crusades from the Nineteenth to the
Twenty-First Century
Engaging the Crusades, Volume One
Edited by Mike Horswell and Jonathan Phillips

The Crusades in the Modern World
Engaging the Crusades, Volume Two
Edited by Mike Horswell and Akil N. Awan

For more information about this series, please visit https://www.routledge.
com/Engaging-the-Crusades/book-series/ETC

The Crusades in the Modern World

Engaging the Crusades, Volume Two

**Edited by Mike Horswell
and Akil N. Awan**

Routledge
Taylor & Francis Group

LONDON AND NEW YORK

First published 2020
by Routledge
2 Park Square, Milton Park, Abingdon, Oxon OX14 4RN

and by Routledge
605 Third Avenue, New York, NY 10017

First issued in paperback 2021

Routledge is an imprint of the Taylor & Francis Group, an informa business

Publisher's Note
The publisher has gone to great lengths to ensure the quality of this reprint but points out that some imperfections in the original copies may be apparent.

British Library Cataloguing-in-Publication Data
A catalogue record for this book is available from the British Library

Library of Congress Cataloging-in-Publication Data
A catalog record has been requested for this book

ISBN 13: 978-1-03-209188-4 (pbk)
ISBN 13: 978-1-138-06607-6 (hbk)

Typeset in Times New Roman
by codeMantra

Contents

x   *Contents*

Figures

Acknowledgements

The second volume in *Engaging the Crusades* under the remit of 'what are the crusades today?' has come together coherently to offer a strong continuation of the work begun in September 2015. This is in no small part to the contributors whose patience, willingness to engage with the editorial process, and insight has made this volume both possible and an important next step for the series. Mike would, as ever, like to thank Lauren for her forbearance, laughter and support.

Abbreviations

APF   Alliance for Peace and Freedom
CUP   Cambridge University Press
DN   *Democracia Nacional*
MUP   Manchester University Press
OUP   Oxford University Press
PNR   *Partido Nacional Renovador*
PP   *Partido Popular*

Frequently used references:

CPOV	Geert Lovink and Nathaniel Tkacz, eds., *Critical Point of View: A Wikipedia Reader* (Amsterdam: Institute of Network Cultures, 2011).
Knobler, 'Holy Wars'	Adam Knobler, 'Holy Wars, Empires, and the Portability of the Past: The Modern Uses of Medieval Crusades', *Comparative Studies in Society and History* 48 (2006), pp. 293–325.
Gabriele, 'Debating the "Crusade"'	Matthew Gabriele, 'Debating the "Crusade" in Contemporary America', *The Mediaeval Journal* 6:1 (2016), pp. 73–92.
Heng, 'Holy War Redux'	Geraldine Heng, 'Holy War Redux: The Crusades, Futures of the Past, and Strategic Logic in the "Clash" of Religions', *PMLA* 126:2 (2011), pp. 422–31.
Horswell, *British Crusader Medievalism*	Mike Horswell, *The Rise and Fall of British Crusader Medievalism, c. 1825–1945* (Abingdon: Routledge, 2018).

Engaging the Crusades, Vol. 1	Mike Horswell and Jonathan Phillips, eds., *Perceptions of the Crusades from the Nineteenth to the Twenty-First Century: Engaging the Crusades, Volume One* (Abingdon: Routledge, 2018).
Phillips, *Holy Warriors*	Jonathan Phillips, *Holy Warriors: A Modern History of the Crusades* (London: Vintage, 2010).
Siberry, *New Crusaders*	Elizabeth Siberry, *The New Crusaders: Images of the Crusades in the 19th and Early 20th Centuries* (Aldershot: Ashgate, 2000).
Tyerman, *Debate*	Christopher Tyerman, *The Debate on the Crusades* (Manchester: MUP, 2011).
Wollenburg, 'New Knighthood'	Daniel Wollenberg, 'The New Knighthood: Terrorism and the Medieval', *postmedieval* 5 (2014), pp. 21–33.

Contributors

Akil N. Awan is a Senior Lecturer in Modern History, Political Violence and Terrorism at Royal Holloway, University of London. He is interested in the history of terrorism, radicalisation, social movements, protest and new media. He has written widely, in both academic and popular contexts, including. *Radicalisation and Media: Terrorism and Connectivity in the New Media Ecology* (2011), *Jihadism Transformed: al-Qaeda and Islamic State's Global Battle of Ideas* (2016), and *The Cambridge Companion to Radicalisation* (forthcoming). He is Founder and Chair of the Political Science Association's Specialist Group on Political Violence & Terrorism. He is on Twitter: @Akil_N_Awan.

Marco Giardini obtained a PhD in Medieval History at the University of Milan in 2011. His research interests cover the manifold manifestation of eschatological and apocalyptic expectations between the Middle Ages and early modern ages, with special references to their legendary and literary developments (see the monograph entitled *Figure del regno nascosto: Le leggende del Prete Gianni e delle dieci tribù perdute d'Israele fra Medioevo e prima età moderna*). He is currently post-doctorand in Religious Sciences at the École Pratique des Hautes Études in Paris.

Mike Horswell completed his PhD at Royal Holloway, University of London, and his book – *The Rise and Fall of British Crusader Medievalism, c.1825–1945* – was published in 2018. He has taught at Royal Holloway, King's College London, and the University of Oxford and is currently researching, teaching and writing about the memory and use of the crusades in the modern era.

Phil James is a PhD candidate at Royal Holloway, University of London. When he isn't exploring the crusading credentials of

Mexican criminal organisations, his main area of research interest is the engagement with crusading ideas in the early modern period, with a particular focus on late seventeenth-century Poland and the 1683 Relief of Vienna.

Rachael Pymm is an independent scholar from Surrey, UK. She holds an MA in Crusader Studies from Royal Holloway, University of London, and has been researching the ways in which the medieval crusades have been depicted on postage stamps. Her work on the mythology and purported medical and magical applications of snakestones has been published in *Geology and Medicine: Historical Connections* by the Geological Society, London, and in the journal *Folklore*.

Hilary Rhodes recently completed her PhD in medieval studies at the University of Leeds, where she taught in the School of History for several years. She works primarily on crusading history, medieval gender, social, and queer history; medieval and modern historiography; and the function of the 'imagined medieval'. She can be contacted at h.m.rhodes@leeds.ac.uk.

Tiago João Queimada e Silva is a PhD candidate from the University of Turku (Finland), where he is currently preparing a dissertation titled 'Portrayals of an Encounter with Islam: Christian-Muslim Interaction in Medieval Portuguese Historiography'. He holds a master's degree in History of the Middle Ages from the University of Coimbra (Portugal) and has recently been researching and writing about depictions of Christian-Muslim interaction in medieval Portuguese chronicles and genealogical records.

Susanna A. Throop is an Associate Professor and Department Chair of History at Ursinus College (U.S.A.). She is the author of *Crusading as an Act of Vengeance, 1095–1216* (2011) and *The Crusades: An Epitome* (2018) and co-editor of *Vengeance in the Middle Ages: Emotion, Religion and Feud* (2010) and *The Crusades and Visual Culture* (2015).

Introduction
The crusades in the modern world

Mike Horswell and Akil N. Awan

The crusades refuse to remain in the past: icons of continuing Western imperialist aggression for some, for others they represent a foundational stage of a coherent Christian Europe defined against the Islamic East. Regularly employed to support violence, the crusades have been cited as providing inspiration and warning since their practical organisation waned, and the idea of crusading continues to fuel polemics to the present.[1] Their meaning for today is contested, mutable and heterogeneous.

This volume interrogates perceptions of the crusades and crusading, which are common currency in the twenty-first century through a selection of uses. The authors here each demonstrate how these perceptions of the crusades are deployed in causes and conflicts that mark the present, and in so doing, they contribute to the work of historicising and contextualising their use. In asking 'how are these images created?' and 'what are they designed to do?', contributors foreground ways in which perceptions of the crusades are constructed, deployed and received.

The selected topics are complementary rather than definitive; they illustrate the potential of the field and start conversations about how the crusades and crusading are perceived in our contemporary world. The perspectives are skewed Westward, thus highlighting the need for analyses that problematise a monolithic 'Eastern' or 'Islamic' view of the crusades and reflect the expertise of the scholars assembled and the limitations of space. The breadth of topics and material included – jihadi fantasies to papal apologies, Senegalese stamps to Mexican cartel propaganda, academic historiography to Wikipedia – is united by crusader medievalism, and fruitful cross-pollination comes from bringing these studies together. Indeed, strands of crusading interpretation and concern reoccur.

Most prominently, and perhaps most pressingly, the appropriation of the crusades to justify extremist violence, particularly by jihadists like al-Qaeda and Islamic State, is explored here by Akil Awan and complemented by the work of Tiago Silva, Hilary Rhodes and Phil James. Crusading provides rhetorical veneers for ideological constructs that thrive on polarised positions and hard binary identities. Building on this analysis, notably the construction of oppositional identities, Tiago Silva's contribution to this volume considers the use of the rhetoric of 'Reconquista' in far-right discourses in Spain, Portugal and, more broadly, in Europe. The crusades – blended seamlessly here into the myth of a Christian Iberian *Reconquista* – serve contemporary political and social agendas of exclusion and blame. Hilary Rhodes reflects on American investment in crusader medievalism – both rhetoric and imagined realities – and revisits the 2005 Ridley Scott film *Kingdom of Heaven* to unpack what was revealed by its reception and afterlife as an iconic popular presentation of the crusades and image of Saladin. Rhodes shows that the film's version of Saladin has broad resonance: images of the Kurdish Muslim leader have found their way into the recruiting images of Islamic fundamentalists online. Phil James' chapter on the use of the Knights Templar, the medieval military order, by a Mexican drug cartel demonstrates that the twelfth-century Rule of the Templars is sufficiently flexible to serve as a framing device for unexpected identity-construction and discipline.

These threads are taken up in Marco Giardini's chapter on the memory of the crusades in twentieth-century Catholicism in which he identifies a polarisation of interpretation of the crusades and crusading. This fracture runs along a 'progressive'/'traditionalist' fault line represented by the reception of the Second Vatican Council (1962–65) and subsequent reforming initiatives. Here, the entanglement of attitudes to the crusades with perceptions of the Middle Ages is clear and is a theme Susanna Throop advances in her chapter. In contextualising crusader studies amongst current conversations about the future of medieval studies, the role of higher education, and the reception and use of academic histories by white nationalists, Throop returns to appropriations of the crusades by contemporary extremists and the implications for scholars of the crusades today.

Other themes interwoven in earlier chapters are brought out with greater clarity later in the volume. Rachael Pymm's contribution considers stamps as projections of national identity; images that convey meaning quickly about what the crusades were and what they mean. In so doing, reference is again made to the twentieth-century Spanish dictator Franco's use of crusading and papal interactions with the crusading past, which links Silva and Giardini's chapters, and national appropriations of the crusades – the subject of a forthcoming volume in this series.

Building on Rhodes' call that historians 'must have an awareness of the discourse they are contributing to and the legacy in which they are operating, as well as an acknowledgment of its consequences', Throop's chapter points to the embodied, presentist nature of knowledge of the past and clarifies an ethical imperative. The crusades are researched, taught and received by people with social, political and cultural orientations that cannot be escaped. All action, all academic work, has ethical implications; the question, Throop asks, is to what ends are those actions being directed. The relationship of academic scholarship to popular perceptions of the crusades is picked up in several chapters, not least those of Silva, Giardini and Throop, and is a core theme of Mike Horswell's consideration of the culturally ubiquitous Wikipedia's presentation of the crusades. Coupling evaluation of the discussion pages with historicising the 'Crusades' article renders visible both the information presented and the social aspects active in the processes of its creation.

The crusades today, then, are informed by historian's creations of the past, moderated and negotiated by present political and theological fields of mobilisation. These perceptions are presented as information ('the crusades were...'), as entertainment, and for mobilisation: clearly, we see that ideas of crusading continue to carry cultural currency today.

Note

1 See Heng, 'Holy War Redux'; Gabriele, 'Debating the "Crusade"'; Wollenberg, 'New Knighthood'.

1   Weaponising the crusades

Justifying terrorism and political violence

Akil N. Awan

On 29 October 2010, a young woman entered the FedEx courier company's Sana'a office and dispatched a parcel to a synagogue in Chicago, Illinois. Contained within the package was a potent explosive device disguised as a printer cartridge, designed to detonate over U.S. airspace. Fortuitously, the bomb was safely intercepted en route at a scheduled stopover. Responsibility for the thwarted attack was quickly claimed by the Yemen-based franchise of the al-Qaeda terrorist network, al-Qaeda in the Arabian Peninsula (AQAP).

Lost amidst the flurry of security activity, and the understandably palpable sense of relief over the disrupted plot, however, was one incongruous overlooked detail. The package was addressed to a man who had been dead for over 800 years. The bomb's intended recipient was 'Reynald Krak',[1] a pseudonym for Raynald of Châtillon – the infamous twelfth-century Frankish knight, who notoriously plundered Muslim caravans and killed Muslim pilgrims, even in periods of truce during the Second Crusade. The Muslim scholar, Baha ad-Din ibn Shaddad, renowned for his biography of Saladin and a contemporary of Raynald, alluded to his notoriety by describing him as a 'monstrous infidel and terrible oppressor'.[2] Indeed, in the wake of the Battle of Hattin (1187), the victorious Saladin himself differentiated his treatment of crusader captives on the basis of their reputations. Whereas Guy of Lusignan was magnanimously offered a cup of iced rose water, the widely despised Raynald was beheaded by Saladin's own hand. In the centuries since Hattin, Raynald became a reviled caricature of cruelty and violence in both the East and the West; a bogeyman, personifying the crusades' enduring legacy of Christian-Muslim enmity.[3]

Raynald of Châtillon may have been dead for close to a millennium, but the ghost of his memory had been revived to chilling effect. AQAP's glossy English-language magazine, *Inspire*, explained the group's strange choice of 'target' for its terrorist attack:

We are fighting a war against American tyranny. This is a new Crusade waged by the West against Islam. [...] This current battle fought by the West is not an isolated battle but is a continuation of a long history of aggression by the West against the Muslim world. In order to revive and bring back this history we listed the name of Reynald Krak [...] who was one of the worst and most treacherous of the Crusade's leaders. [...] Today we are facing a coalition of Crusaders and Zionists and [...] this operation is a response to the Crusaders aggression against the Muslims.[4]

Terrorism, as Alex Schmid and Jenny De Graaf's seminal work on the subject explains, is best understood, if it is viewed in the first instance as communication, rather than as mere violence.[5] Thus, AQAP's decision to resurrect a long-dead crusader as their imaginary interlocutor in their political communication with the West should not have surprised anyone – particularly as the crusades have long symbolised *the* seminal conflict that defined the troubled relationship between Western Christendom and the Muslim World; a toxic legacy that continues to the present day. This chapter explores the ways in which the problematic legacy of the crusades has been employed by jihadists today to further their political aims, foment social divisions and ultimately legitimise violence and terrorism.

Constructing grand narratives

Central to the worldview of many extremist groups is the presence of what Jean-François Lyotard referred to as a grand or meta-narrative.[6] Grand narratives are overarching, totalising accounts or meta-discourses, which provide ideologies with a legitimating philosophy of history. Essentially, these accounts claim to connect and give meaning to disparate historical events, experiences and phenomena by appealing to some universal, overarching schema. Under the rubric of the grand narrative, extremists work to construct stories that allow them to connect their imagined past, present and future, thus enabling them to make sense of the world around them and locate their place within history. In the process, these narratives function to legitimise power, authority and broader worldviews, often hiding political motives and acts, such as violence, behind the façade of lofty ideals.

Jihadists have long sought to construct and deploy a particularly tendentious grand narrative in order to support and validate their worldview. One of the most significant and recurring refrains within this narrative is the construction of the crusades – not simply as a series of eight historical campaigns that took place between the eleventh and thirteenth centuries – but rather as a central existential threat; a label ubiquitously applied to any form of Western aggression and encroachment against the Islamic world throughout history.

At first glance, this may seem surprising, considering that the early crusading expeditions were largely neglected by contemporary Muslim chroniclers, who viewed the invaders as primitive, uncouth, barbarians who posed little concern.[7] Indeed, the Islamic world's initial response to the crusades was one of 'apathy, compromise and preoccupation with internal problems'.[8] Moreover, beyond the actual events themselves, the memory of the crusades played a considerably less significant part in Islamic conceptions of history from the fourteenth to the nineteenth centuries, than is often assumed.[9] This should not surprise us, considering that the crusades had not been of the Muslims' making, and which on balance, the crusaders had lost; the Muslim world had ultimately proved successful in repelling the crusades, reclaiming any territorial gains made by Western Christendom and having destroyed any lingering crusader presence along the Levantine Mediterranean coast. Indeed, throughout this entire period, there was no Arabic word for the crusades per se,[10] and the crusades were simply subsumed within a broader history of recurrent waves of aggression by the *Faranj* or Franks.

It was not until the mid-nineteenth century that the terms *harb al-salib* (the war of the cross) and *al-salibiyyun* (crusaders) entered the Arabic lexicon and, even then, only through an appropriation of European terms encountered in European history books. This development was largely in response to an assertive, expansionist Europe who now threatened the sovereignty and territorial integrity of the Ottoman empire, plunging it into crisis. The first Arabic history of the crusades, *al-Akhbar al-saniyya fi'l-hurub al-salibiyya* (*Great Accounts in the Crusading Wars*), penned by the Egyptian historian Sayyid Ali al-Hariri was not published until 1899. Al-Hariri echoing the sentiments of the earlier French historian, Joseph François Michaud, viewed the crusades as a forerunner to European colonialism. It was precisely at the moment that Michaud had been writing his seminal six-volume *Histoire des Croisades*, that France had embarked on its colonising invasion of Algeria in 1830. It was in this context that both politicians and historians began to proudly identify the new colonising movement and its *mission civilisatrice* with the crusades of old.[11]

The Ottoman Caliph, Sultan Abdul Hamid II (r. 1876–1909), presciently recognising the political utility of this framing language, lamented the new European 'crusade' against the Ottoman empire – a view al-Hariri went on to endorse in his book:

> The sovereigns of Europe nowadays attack our Sublime Empire in a manner bearing a great resemblance to the deeds of those people [the crusaders] in bygone times. Our most glorious sultan, Abdul Hamid II, has rightly remarked that Europe is now carrying out a Crusade against us in the form of a political campaign.[12]

In the century that followed, the moribund Ottoman empire was dismembered in the wake of the First World War, the caliphate was abolished, and virtually every Muslim majority country was either colonised outright or came under the sphere of influence of European powers. Even after the end of European empire in the latter half of the twentieth century, unequal power dynamics continued to dominate the relationships between the Islamic world and their old colonial masters, whose influence had now also been bolstered by an increasingly assertive U.S.A. It is in this context that we might begin to understand the potency of crusading discourse in the wider jihadist meta-narrative. For jihadists, the memory of the crusades lives on as the clearest example of an assertive, belligerent Christianity, an early harbinger of aggression and imperialism of the Christian West to come.[13]

The Egyptian radical, Said Qutb, often regarded as the leading theorist-architect of salafi-jihadism,[14] was the first to systematically invoke the crusades within the broader Islamist grand narrative. Born into the heady political milieu of a British-occupied Egypt in 1906, Qutb witnessed first-hand, the subjugation of both his native country, and the wider Middle East and North Africa (MENA) region, being ravaged by unchecked European hegemony. Seething in humiliation, he wrote of European colonialism as nothing more than a mask for the enduring 'crusading spirit':[15]

> But from that time [of the Crusaders] to this, [Islam] has to contend with ferocious enemies of the same spirit as the Crusaders, enemies both open and hidden. The spirit of the Crusades, though perhaps in a milder form, still hangs over Europe; and that civilisation in its dealings with the Islamic world still occupies a position that bears clear traces of that genocidal force. The Crusader spirit that runs in the blood of all Occidentals […] colors their thinking, [and] is responsible for their imperialistic fear of the spirit of Islam and for their efforts to crush the strength of Islam.[16]

Al-Qaeda and the 'Zionist-Crusader' enemy

Virtually, every Islamist radical since Qutb has adopted this framing vis-à-vis the crusades, including, and most significantly, al-Qaeda. Consequently, the outmoded nineteenth-century paradigm drawing an equivalency between the crusades and European colonialism only survives principally within the twentieth- and twenty-first-centuries jihadist mind-set and grand narrative. In a letter to Al-Jazeera in November 2001, bin Laden wrote:

> Is it a single, unrelated event, or is it part of a long series of Crusader wars against the Islamic world? Since World War One, which ended over 83 years ago, the entire Islamic world has fallen under the Crusader banners, under the British, French, and Italian governments. They divided up the whole world between them, and Palestine fell into the hands of the British.[17]

For these groups, all contemporary conflicts raging in the Muslim world, from the 'War on Terror' to ethno-nationalist conflicts, are refracted through the prism of a wider historical global attack on Islam and Muslims by a belligerent 'Zionist-Crusader Alliance'. As bin Laden claimed in 1996:

> The people of Islam had suffered from aggression, iniquity and injustice imposed on them by the Zionist-Crusaders alliance and their collaborators [...]. Their blood was spilled in Palestine and Iraq. [...] Massacres in Tajikistan, Burma, Kashmir, Assam, Philippine, Fatani, Ogadin, Somalia, Eritrea, Chechnya and in Bosnia-Herzegovina took place, massacres that send shivers in the body and shake the conscience.[18]

The distillation of a common enemy from this diverse array of geopolitical conflicts and actors, as an anachronistic 'Zionist-Crusader Alliance', has been central to the jihadist aim of presenting a Manichean, us-and-them, dichotomy. Indeed, one of al-Qaeda's earliest and most important statements to the outside world in 1998 was presented under the auspices of the *World Islamic Front for Jihad Against Jews and Crusaders*. The 'World Islamic Front' in fact represented no such thing, and in addition to bin Laden and his deputy Ayman al-Zawahiri was constituted of three relatively unimportant leaders from Egypt, Pakistan and Bangladesh, but nevertheless represented a self-aggrandising projection of how al-Qaeda wished to see themselves and be seen by others.

In response to this 'Zionist-Crusader' assault, the jihadists claimed not only to have awakened the global Muslim community of belief, or *Ummah*, to the existential threat posed by the neo-crusaders but also to serve as the sole and crucial vanguard, helping mobilise Muslim audiences to respond to this historic enemy in kind: 'Our goal is for our nation to unite in the face of the Christian crusade. This is the fiercest battle. Muslims have never faced anything bigger than this'.[19] Crusader rhetoric has been central to the construction of jihadists' own self-perceptions too. In facing this enemy, jihadists have long sought to portray themselves as chivalrous medieval knights, at the head of the vanguard, heroically resisting these new incursions into the Muslim heartlands by the 'neo-crusaders'. The appeal to the valiant holy warrior or chivalrous knight is a recurring trope in much jihadist literature, with Ayman al-Zawahiri's famous text, *Fursan Taht Rayah Al-Nabi* (*Knights Under the Prophet's Banner*), written around 2001, representing one of the earliest and most important examples.[20]

The potency of the jihadist's alluringly simple meta-narrative has been bolstered by the stark and unflinching certainty of its interpretational framework that has remained remarkably coherent and consistent over time.[21] Some have even argued that al-Qaeda has been eminently successful in persuading Muslim audiences to accept their distorted grand narratives and historical revisionism.[22] Indeed, even their ideological opponents have recognised the jihadists manifest success in promulgating this historicised reading of contemporary events, with Michael Scheuer, the ex-head of the Central Intelligence Agency (CIA) 'bin Laden unit', referring to Osama bin Laden as a 'modern Saladin [...] [who] makes brilliant use of the intimacy of Muslims with Islamic history'.[23]

But possibly the greatest strength of the jihadists meta-narrative is that their Manichean worldview of believers and infidels, of jihad and crusade, is reflected, and indeed inadvertently corroborated, by the equally diametrically opposing dichotomy offered by their opponents, from the infamous Bush dictum 'you're either with us or against us in the fight against terror',[24] to Huntington's 'clash of civilisations' thesis.[25] However, perhaps nothing has epitomised this reciprocity of legitimation better than President George W. Bush's infamous and unfortunate characterisation of the 'War in Terror' as a new 'crusade'. Choosing to adopt overtly religious rhetoric shortly after 9/11, he vowed to 'rid the world of evil-doers', cautioning that 'this crusade, this war on terrorism, is going to take a while'.[26] In response, bin Laden leapt at the chance to employ his opponent's words in validating his own worldview:

> Bush stated that the world has to be divided in two: Bush and his supporters, and any country that doesn't get into the global crusade is with the terrorists. Bush said it in his own words: "crusade". When Bush says that, they try to cover up for him, then he said he didn't mean it. He said "crusade". Bush divided the world into two: "either with us or with terrorism". Bush is the leader; he carries the big cross and walks.[27]

Bin Laden returned once again to this incongruous synergy in his 2004 *Message to the American People*, arguing that 'it seems as if we and the White House are on the same team' and that this 'truly shows that al-Qaida has made gains, but on the other hand it also shows that the Bush administration has likewise profited'.[28]

This binary framing has been so central to the jihadist worldview that when bin Laden was asked by a journalist immediately in the wake of 9/11, how al-Qaeda could possibly contemplate defeating the U.S. military behemoth, his response mandated that he reconfigure the battle lines first: 'This battle is not between al-Qaeda and the U.S. This is a battle of Muslims against the global crusaders'.[29] Indeed, so potent have these imagined polarised identities become, that their propagators can go to seemingly absurd lengths to sustain them, as the Islamic State (IS) group does here, by subsuming decidedly non-Christian nations like Arab countries and Japan under the crusader rubric:

> What is Japan's concern with us? [...] It is yet another crusade just like the former crusades led by Richard the Lionheart, Barbarossa of Germany, and Louis of France. Likewise today, when Bush raised the cross, the crusader countries immediately scrambled. What is the Arab countries' concern with this crusade? [...] Because they are pleased with the rule of the cross.[30]

IS's magazine also reinforced this imagery with a photograph of murdered Japanese journalist Kenji Goto, kneeling in an orange jumpsuit beside his executioner immediately prior to his beheading in 2015. Below the image was the patently absurd title, 'The Japanese Crusader

THE JAPANESE CRUSADER KENJI GOTO JOGO

Figure 1.1 'The Japanese Crusader Kenji Goto Jogo', *Dabiq*, Issue 7, 2015.

Kenji Goto Jogo' (see Figure 1.1). It was this same perverse logic at play that branded Muath al-Kasasbeh, a Jordanian Muslim pilot captured and burned to death in 2015 after his fighter aircraft crashed over Syria, a 'Jordanian crusader pilot'.[31]

IS and the resurrection of the 'caliphate'

Crusading rhetoric has also been yoked to the state-building project of the IS and the nascent statelets that preceded it. Abu Bakr Naji's *Management of Savagery* (*Idārat at-Tawaḥḥuš*) – perhaps the most important jihadist stratagem on creating an IS, invokes the historical examples of the crusades to reinforce its central thesis on state building. Naji argues that the most important medieval Muslim victory against the Crusaders at the Battle of Hattin (1187) was not solely the result of epic decisive battles between the two forces, but rather was the culmination of a longer strategy of attrition by smaller forces.[32] The purpose of this historical analogy was to clearly identify the various jihadist groups at the time of Naji's writing (c. 2004), with the small bands and factions of the medieval period who were instrumental in laying the groundwork for Saladin's eventual victory over the crusaders.

For many years, al-Qaeda had invoked an aspirational future caliphate – the religio-political entity that had historically governed the Muslim world – as their utopian end goal. On 29 June 2014, abetted by the insecurity and tumult in the wake of the Arab uprisings and the war in Iraq, a relatively new jihadist offshoot group calling itself the Islamic State of Iraq and the Levant (IS), hijacked this narrative by brazenly announced the re-establishment of the caliphate, turning al-Qaeda's abstract utopia into a dystopic reality whilst al-Qaeda's leadership could only look on in dumbfounded impotence: 'As for you, oh soldiers of the Islamic State, then congratulations to you. Congratulations on this clear victory [...] Now the caliphate has returned, humbling the necks of the enemy'.[33]

IS's so-called caliphate was short-lived, having lost all territorial gains by March 2019. Nevertheless, whilst it existed, the caliphate straddled vast swathes of Iraq and Syria, governing close to the ten million people within its realm as an atavistic throwback, that positively revelled in barbaric savagery and violence, all whilst shrouded in the language and regalia of historic caliphs and religious piety.

Whilst this period represented a new era for jihadism, IS were keen to stake their claim as the rightful new heirs to the jihadist mantle, and so retained a strong sense of continuity with the earliest jihadist grand narrative. Nowhere was this more apparent than in their invocation of a tendentious historical narrative; a curious amalgam of nostalgia for an imagined past and teleological apocalyptic imagery. A pertinent example of the nexus of IS's eschatology and historical revisionism can be seen in the choice of name for their flagship, glossy

English-language magazine, *Dabiq*, named after a small Syrian town, close to the Turkish border.

The town of Dabiq, whilst being of negligible strategic importance, was nevertheless the site of a fiercely contested battle, waged by IS fighters, who fought zealously to capture what they believed was prophesised to be the final battleground between the Muslims and Rome (Byzantium). In this case, the Romans were interpreted to be the Americans and their allies. The *Dabiq* editorial team explained the publication's name from an Islamic eschatological perspective: 'The area [Dabiq] will play a historical role in the battles leading up to the conquests of Constantinople, then Rome',[34] ultimately heralding the Day of Judgement. The rather inconvenient fact that Constantinople had been under Muslim sovereignty since the time of Ottoman Sultan Mehmed II, who had himself conquered it from IS's 'Rome' (Byzantium) in 1453, should have raised alarms over this decidedly tenuous interpretation.

Nevertheless, following the decisive victory at Dabiq in August 2014, jubilant IS supporters tweeted pictures of their flag, fluttering atop a hill overlooking Dabiq, alongside quotes from the prophecy. In the following months, as the U.S.A. began to contemplate military options against IS, supporters became positively ecstatic over the prospect of facing the neo-crusaders in a final apocalyptic battle: 'the foreign invasion of northern Syria, meaning from the plain of Dabiq. The battles (of the End Times) have grown near', and 'In Dabiq the crusade will end'.[35]

Much of IS's media output continued to reference the prophecy in subsequent months by citing the now familiar refrain, 'The spark has been lit here in Iraq, and its heat will continue to intensify [...] until it burns the crusader armies in Dabiq' (see Figure 1.2).[36] Dabiq remained an important part of IS's perverse apocalypticism until 2016. The video beheading of American aid worker and former U.S. Army ranger, Peter Kassig, in November 2014, for example, was meticulously staged and filmed with Dabiq prominently featured as its backdrop. The killer – a sinister, balaclava-clad British fighter known as 'Jihadi John' – wielding a hunting knife by Kassig's decapitated corpse, addressed the camera in a quintessentially London accent: 'Here we are, burying the first American Crusader in Dabiq, eagerly waiting for the remainder of your armies to arrive'.[37]

Crusading imagery remained a prominent feature of the IS's propaganda efforts. Issue 4 of *Dabiq*, released in October 2014, for example, was entitled *The Failed Crusade* and contained the feature length article 'Reflections on the Final Crusade' (see Figure 1.3). In a striking

Figure 1.2 'Until it burns the crusader armies in Dabiq', *Dabiq*, Issue 1, 2014.

illustration of the anachronism represented by IS's worldview, the magazine quoted its spokesman Mohammed al-Adnani's infamous threat against 'Rome's Crusaders':

> We will conquer your Rome, break your crosses, and enslave your women, by the permission of Allah, the Exalted. If we do not reach that time, then our children and grandchildren will reach it, and they will sell your sons as slaves at the slave market.[38]

To reinforce the point, the front-cover image also featured a photoshopped IS flag fluttering atop the Holy See in the Vatican. A later issue of *Dabiq*, repeated almost verbatim, bin Laden's earlier warning: 'It is yet another crusade just like the former crusades led by Richard the Lionheart, Barbarossa of Germany, and Louis of France. Likewise today, when Bush raised the cross, the crusader countries immediately scrambled'.[39]

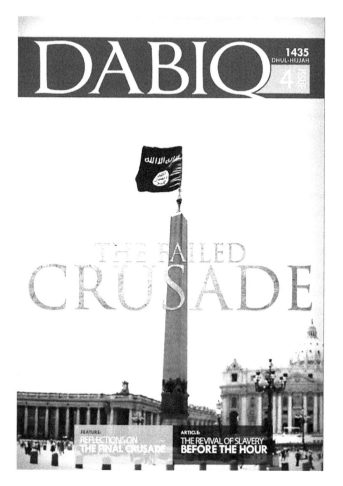

Figure 1.3 'The Failed Crusade' (Front cover) *Dabiq*, Issue 4 (2014).

IS continued to invoke the spectre of the crusades in its various propaganda efforts, even introducing the paradoxical term 'Crusader "civilian"', to sanction the murder of non-combatants in Western countries:

> Will you leave the American, the Frenchman, or any of their allies to walk safely upon the earth while the armies of the crusaders strike the lands of the Muslims not differentiating between a civilian and fighter?[40]

Having established an apparent equivalency, the article implored that 'every Muslim should get out of his house, find a crusader, and kill him'.[41] In October 2016, *Rumiyah* ratcheted up these attempts to instigate autonomous 'lone wolf' style terrorist attacks in the West as a way of compensating for military losses in their core territory: 'Let them follow the example of the lions who have preceded them by striking the Crusader citizens and interests wherever they are found in the West'.[42]

Following the deadly terrorist attacks in Paris on 13 November 2015, IS propaganda justified their attack by referring to France as 'the lead carrier of the cross in Europe', claiming their fighters had 'cast terror into the hearts of the crusaders in their very own homeland'. The statement attempted to defend their attack on the Stade de France football stadium, by arguing that it was chosen as it was hosting a match 'between the teams of Germany and France, both of which are crusader nations'. Perhaps most incongruously, the claim posited 'Paris was thereby shaken beneath the crusaders' feet, who were constricted by its streets. The result of the attacks was the deaths of no less than two hundred crusaders and the wounding of even more'.[43] Clearly, if ordinary Parisians, including a great many French Muslims amongst their ranks, could be identified as 'crusaders', then the crusader designation was proved once again to be little more than an expedient label applied to dehumanise victims and enemies alike.

This Manichean dualism that sought to divide the world in two camps – of crusaders and Muslims, also became shockingly evident in the wake of the January 2015 attacks against the offices of Charlie Hebdo. The February issue of *Dabiq* wrote of polarising the world by destroying its greatest threat, the 'grayzone': that liminal space in which young Frenchmen could be both Muslims and good citizens of the Republic, without any inherent contradiction. IS anticipated that provocative terrorist attacks, like the ones in Paris in January and November of 2015, would goad the French towards over-reaction and create a climate of fear and hostility, further alienating French Muslims from wider society and 'further bring division to the world and destroy the grayzone everywhere'. Western Muslims would then be forced to make 'one of two choices': between apostasy or IS's bastardised version of belief (see Figure 1.4). The article ended by citing, rather approvingly, George W. Bush's central dictum: 'The world today is divided into two camps. Bush spoke the truth when he said, "Either you are with us or you are with the terrorists." Meaning, either you are with the crusade or you are with Islam'.[44]

The eminent success of IS's grand narrative can be traced to its ability to connect disparate historical events and experiences within its

Figure 1.4 'From Hypocrisy to Apostasy: The Extinction of the Grayzone' (Front cover), *Dabiq*, Issue 7, 2015.

broader interpretational framework, aligning that historical narrative to geopolitical developments more broadly, and then disseminate that worldview with an incredibly potent twenty-first-century media apparatus. Following the declaration of the establishment of its caliphate in June 2014, the self-anointed caliph Abu Bakr al-Baghdadi declared:

> We have now trespassed the borders that were drawn by the malicious hands in lands of Islam in order to limit our movements and

confine us inside them. And we are working, Allah permitting, to eliminate them [borders]. This blessed advance will not stop until we hit the last nail in the coffin of the Sykes–Picot conspiracy.

Later that same month, IS released a video, *The End of Sykes-Picot*, in which bulldozers symbolically levelled part of the border between eastern Syria and northern Iraq.[45] This was also accompanied by a savvy social media campaign with the hashtag #Sykespicotover.

The border in question was a colonial remnant of the Sykes-Picot Agreement of 1916, made between the French and British empires in the midst of First World War, as they greedily eyed their spoils of war in the shape of the crumbling Ottoman empire. An arbitrary line in the sand, based on a cartographer's typesetting on a colonial map, established the boundaries between the British and French spheres. The French would claim everything to the North of the line and the British to the South. This bizarre line in the sand would go on to become the border between Iraq, Syria and Jordan and laid the foundation for demarcating the borders of these new artificial states in subsequent treaties.[46]

In the wake of the Ottoman empire's dismantlement, the abolition of the caliphate, and the subsequent colonial domination of the Muslim world, the Sykes-Picot Agreement came to serve as useful shorthand for Western treachery and greed, and Muslim humiliation at the behest of colonial machinations. In 2014, *Dabiq* wrote:

> After demolishing the Syrian/Iraqi border set up by the crusaders to divide and disunite the Muslims, and carve up their lands in order to consolidate their control of the region, the mujahidin of the Khilafah delivered yet another blow to nationalism and the Sykes-Picot inspired borders that define it. The establishment of a new wilayah (province), Wilayat al-Furat, was announced this month by the Islamic State in an effort to eliminate any remaining traces of the kufri, nationalistic borders from the hearts of Muslims.[47]

Consequently, the claimed dissolution of Sykes-Picot took on a potent symbolic nature for the group, allowing IS to attempt to position themselves as the only viable post-colonial, post-national, even post-Arab polity: 'The banners of nationalism [...] are oppose[d] to Tawhid and the Shar'iah and represent the kufri and shirki ideologies brought to the Muslim world by the two crusaders: Sykes and Picot'.[48] Moreover, they had demonstrated in some small way, IS's ability to restore a quixotic notion of Muslim unity, despite having been fractured by a century of colonial Western intervention.

In September 2016, following their imminent rout at Dabiq at the hands of Turkish backed Syrian rebel forces, IS quietly ended publication of *Dabiq* and replaced it with a new publication titled *Rumiyah* (Rome), now referencing the Islamic prophecy over the fall of Rome instead. The cynical adaptation of the narrative showed that even worldview-confirming prophesies are not always immune to the vicissitudes of war.

Conclusion

The twenty-first century has witnessed the sharpest escalation of crusading discourses since the crusades themselves ended, becoming a leitmotif within not just the jihadist grand narrative but also the contemporary far-right's worldview.[49] The fact these narratives rest on deliberately ahistorical and highly distorted readings of events, that bear little semblance to earlier understandings and representations of the crusades in both the Muslim world and the West, has done little to curtail their potency or currency. Indeed, what we have witnessed has been nothing short of the weaponising of history, in furtherance of dangerous contemporary political projects. The construction and deployment of these tendentious historical narratives in order to support and validate the worldviews of violent extremists has engendered mutual enmity and the enactment of terrible violence in response.

We might take some small solace in the fact that these tenuous narratives are relatively easy to contest. Both the crusading rhetoric in jihadist propaganda and the very word 'crusade', for example, were largely absent from the Muslim world prior to the mid-nineteenth century. Their resurrection might more aptly be described as an artefact of the humiliation associated with the colonial era, and so are only tenuously connected to the medieval crusades themselves. We might also point to the absurd surfeit of crusader rhetoric in extremist propaganda that leaves the term itself bereft of any real meaning. Issue 10 of *Rumiyah*, for example, contained no less than 60 separate references to the crusades or crusaders. The utility of the term 'crusader' for earlier jihadists like bin Laden and his ilk lays in its ability to conjure up a monolithic, historical, Western, military enemy; the perfect foil against whom Muslim unity could be diametrically opposed. IS's ever-expanding deployment of the term 'crusader' to accommodate and subsume Arab countries, Jordanian pilots, Japanese journalists, French Muslims and citizens more generally has rendered the term farcical, losing any supposed analytical utility it may have previously held.

Perhaps most importantly, those who benefitted the most from these contentious crusading narratives, at least in the jihadists' case, are on the wane. IS is a spent force, and its caliphate dream lies in ruins. By extension, the grand narrative on which the jihadist worldview was predicated has been dealt a devastating blow, profoundly undermining its appeal and power. It may never fully recover.

Notes

1 Mark Mazzetti and Scott Shane, 'In Yemen Bomb Plot, 2 Darkly Historical Inside Jokes', *The New York Times*, 2 November 2010, <https://www.nytimes.com/2010/11/03/world/03terror.html>, [accessed 20 January 2019].
2 D.S. Richards, *The Rare and Excellent History of Saladin or Al-Nawadir Al-Sultaniyya Wa'l-Mahasin Al-Yusufiyya by Baha' Al-Din Ibn Shaddad: Or Al-Nawadir … Ibn Shaddad* (Aldershot, 2002), p. 37.
3 Jeffrey Lee, *God's Wolf: The Life of the Most Notorious of All Crusaders: Reynald de Chatillon* (London, 2016), p. 4.
4 Al-Qaeda in the Arabian Peninsula (2010) *Inspire*, Issue 3.
5 Alex Peter Schmid and Janny de Graaf, *Violence as Communication: Insurgent Terrorism and the Western News Media* (London, 1982).
6 Jean-François Lyotard, *The Postmodern Condition: A Report on Knowledge* (Minneapolis, 1984).
7 Nikita Elisséeff, 'The Reaction of the Syrian Muslims after the Foundation of the First Latin Kingdom of Jerusalem', in *The Crusades: The Essential Readings*, ed. Thomas F. Madden (Oxford, 2002); Francesco Gabrieli, *Arab Historians of the Crusades*, trans. E.J. Costello (London, 1984).
8 Carole Hillenbrand, *The Crusades: Islamic Perspectives* (Edinburgh, 1999), p. 20.
9 Ibid.; John Tolan et al., *Europe and the Islamic World: A History* (Princeton, 2016). For more recent reappraisals of the memory of the crusades in the Arab world prior to the nineteenth century, see Diana Abouali, 'Saladin's Legacy in the Middle East before the Nineteenth Century', *Crusades* 10 (2011), pp. 175–89; Umej Bhatia, *Forgetting Osama Bin Munqidh, Remembering Osama Bin Laden: The Crusades in Modern Muslim Memory* (Singapore, 2008); Jonathan Phillips, *Saladin* (London, 2019).
10 Phillips, *Holy Warriors*, p. 337.
11 Edward Peters, 'Have Muslims in the Middle East Really Remembered the Pain of the Crusades for a Thousand Years?', *History News Network*, 3 May 2003, <https://historynewsnetwork.org/article/1398>, [accessed 20 January 2019].
12 Edward Peters, 'The Firanj Are Coming – Again', *Foreign Policy Research Institue: E-Notes*, 10 December 2004, <https://www.fpri.org/article/2004/12/the-firanj-are-coming-again/>, [accessed 20 January 2019].
13 Tolan et al., *Europe and the Islamic World*, p. ix.

14 Gilles Kepel, *Jihad: The Trail of Political Islam* (Cambridge, MA, 2003); Quintan Wiktorowicz, 'A Genealogy of Radical Islam', *Studies in Conflict & Terrorism* 28:2 (16 February 2005), pp. 75–97.
15 Sayyid Qutb, *Milestones* (Damascus, 1964), p. 160.
16 Sayyid Quṭb, *Social Justice in Islam*, trans. John B. Hardie and Algar Hamid (Oneonta, NY, 1953), pp. 269–75.
17 Bruce B. Lawrence, ed., *Messages to the World: The Statements of Osama Bin Laden* (London, 2005), p. 135.
18 Osama Bin Laden, 'Declaration of War against the Americans Occupying the Land of the Two Holy Places', 1996, <http://www.mideastweb.org/osamabinladen1.htm>, [accessed 20 January 2019].
19 CNN, 'Transcript of Bin Laden's October Interview', CNN.com, 5 February 2002, <http://edition.cnn.com/2002/WORLD/asiapcf/south/02/05/binladen.transcript/>, [accessed 20 January 2019].
20 Akil N. Awan, 'Spurning "This Worldly Life": Terrorism and Martyrdom in Contemporary Britain', in *Martyrdom and Terrorism: Pre-Modern to Contemporary Perspectives*, ed. Dominic Janes (New York, 2014), p. 245.
21 Akil N. Awan, Andrew Hoskins, and Ben O'Loughlin, *Radicalisation and Media: Connectivity and Terrorism in the New Media Ecology* (London, 2011), pp. 25–26.
22 Lawrence Wright, *The Looming Tower: Al-Qaeda and the Road to 9/11*, 1 (New York, 2007); Michael Scheuer, *Imperial Hubris: Why the West Is Losing the War on Terror* (Washington, DC, 2008).
23 Michael Scheuer, *Osama Bin Laden* (New York, 2012), p. 214.
24 CNN, '"You Are Either with Us or against Us"', *CNN.com*, 6 November 2001, <http://edition.cnn.com/2001/US/11/06/gen.attack.on.terror/>, [accessed 20 January 2019].
25 Samuel P. Huntington, *The Clash of Civilizations and the Remaking of World Order* (London, 2002).
26 Peter Waldman and Hugh Pope, '"Crusade" Reference Reinforces Fears War on Terrorism Is against Muslims', *Wall Street Journal*, 21 September 2001, <https://www.wsj.com/articles/SB1001020294332922160>, [accessed 20 January 2019].
27 CNN, 'Transcript'.
28 al-Jazeera, 'Full Transcript of Bin Ladin's Speech', *Aljazeera.com*, 1 November 2004, <https://www.aljazeera.com/archive/2004/11/200849163336457223.html>, [accessed 20 January 2019].
29 CNN, 'Transcript of Bin Laden's October Interview'.
30 IS, *Dabiq*, Issue 7 (2015), p. 3.
31 Ibid., p. 6.
32 Available at: <https://azelin.files.wordpress.com/2010/08/abu-bakr-naji-the-management-of-savagery-the-most-critical-stage-through-which-the-umma-will-pass.pdf>, [accessed 20 January 2019].
33 Abu Muhammad Al-Adnani, 'This is the Promise of Allah', 29 June 2014, <https://news.siteintelgroup.com/Jihadist-News/isis-spokesman-declares-caliphate-rebrands-group-as-islamicstate.html>, [accessed 20 January 2019].
34 William McCants, *The ISIS Apocalypse: The History, Strategy, and Doomsday Vision of the Islamic State* (New York, 2015).

35 William McCants, 'ISIS Fantasies of an Apocalyptic Showdown in Northern Syria', *Brookings* (blog), 3 October 2014, <https://www.brookings.edu/blog/markaz/2014/10/03/isis-fantasies-of-an-apocalyptic-showdown-in-northern-syria/> [accessed 20 January 2019].
36 BBC Monitoring, 'Why Is Dabiq so Important for IS?', 4 October 2016, sec. Middle East, <https://www.bbc.com/news/world-middle-east-30083303>, [accessed 20 January 2019].
37 Ibid.
38 IS, *Dabiq*, Issue 4 (2014).
39 IS, *Dabiq*, Issue 7 (2015), p. 3.
40 IS, *Dabiq*, Issue 4 (2014), p. 9.
41 Ibid., p. 44.
42 IS, *Rumiyah*, Issue 2 (2016), p. 3.
43 14 November 2015 <https://twitter.com/abo_m_50/status/665479953568432128>, [accessed 19 November 2015].
44 Akil N. Awan, 'The Charlie Hebdo Attack: The Double Alienation Dilemma', *The National Interest*, 13 January 2015, <http://nationalinterest.org/feature/the-charlie-hebdo-attack-the-double-alienation-dilemma-12021>, [accessed: 20 January 2019].
45 Al-Hayat Media Centre, 'The End of Sykes-Picot', video, 2014.
46 Akil N. Awan, 'Architects of Failure: 100 Years of Sykes-Picot', *History Today*, May 2016, <https://www.historytoday.com/architects-failure-100-years-sykes-picot>, [accessed 20 January 2019].
47 'The Revival of Slavery Before the Hour', *Dabiq*, Issue 4 (2014) p. 17.
48 IS, *Dabiq*, Issue 8 (2015), p. 4.
49 The far-right's use of crusading discourses is beyond the remit of this chapter, but see, Matthew Gabriele, 'Islamophobes Want to Recreate the Crusades. But They Don't Understand Them at All', *Washington Post: PostEverything Perspective*, 7 November 2018, <https://www.washingtonpost.com/posteverything/wp/2017/06/06/islamophobes-want-to-recreate-the-crusades-but-they-dont-understand-them-at-all/>, [accessed 20 January 2019].

Bibliography

al-Jazeera. 'Full Transcript of Bin Ladin's Speech'. *Aljazeera.com*, 1 November 2004. www.aljazeera.com/archive/2004/11/200849163336457223.html. [Accessed 20 December 2018].

Awan, Akil N. 'Architects of Failure: 100 Years of Sykes-Picot'. *History Today*, May 2016. www.historytoday.com/architects-failure-100-years-sykes-picot. [Accessed 20 January 2019].

———. 'Spurning "This Worldly Life": Terrorism and Martyrdom in Contemporary Britain.' In *Martyrdom and Terrorism: Pre-Modern to Contemporary Perspectives*, ed. Dominic Janes. New York: OUP, 2014.

———. 'The Charlie Hebdo Attack: The Double Alienation Dilemma'. *The National Interest*, 13 January 2015. http://nationalinterest.org/feature/the-charlie-hebdo-attack-the-double-alienation-dilemma-12021. [Accessed 20 January 2019].

Awan, Akil N., Andrew Hoskins, and Ben O'Loughlin. *Radicalisation and Media: Connectivity and Terrorism in the New Media Ecology*. London: Routledge, 2011.

BBC Monitoring. 'Why Is Dabiq So Important for IS?', 4 October 2016, sec. Middle East. www.bbc.com/news/world-middle-east-30083303. [Accessed 20 January 2019].

CNN. 'Transcript of Bin Laden's October Interview'. *CNN.com*, 5 February 2002. http://edition.cnn.com/2002/WORLD/asiapcf/south/02/05/binladen. transcript/. [Accessed 20 January 2019].

———. '"You Are Either with Us or against Us"'. *CNN.com*, 6 November 2001. http://edition.cnn.com/2001/US/11/06/gen.attack.on.terror/. [Accessed 20 January 2019].

Elisséeff, Nikita. 'The Reaction of the Syrian Muslims after the Foundation of the First Latin Kingdom of Jerusalem'. In *The Crusades: The Essential Readings*, ed. Thomas F. Madden. Oxford: Blackwell, 2002.

Gabriele, Matthew. 'Islamophobes Want to Recreate the Crusades. But They Don't Understand Them at All'. *Washington Post: PostEverything Perspective*, 7 November 2018. www.washingtonpost.com/posteverything/ wp/2017/06/06/islamophobes-want-to-recreate-the-crusades-but-they-dont-understand-them-at-all/. [Accessed 20 January 2019].

Gabrieli, Francesco. *Arab Historians of the Crusades*. Trans. E.J. Costello. London: Routledge & Kegan, 1984.

Hillenbrand, Carole. *The Crusades: Islamic Perspectives*. Edinburgh: Edinburgh University Press, 1999.

Huntington, Samuel P. *The Clash of Civilizations and the Remaking of World Order*. London: Free Press, 2002.

Kepel, Gilles. *Jihad: The Trail of Political Islam*. Cambridge, MA: Harvard University Press, 2003.

Laden, Osama Bin. 'Declaration of War against the Americans Occupying the Land of the Two Holy Places', 1996. www.mideastweb.org/osamabinladen1. htm. [Accessed 20 January 2019].

Lawrence, Bruce B., ed. *Messages to the World: The Statements of Osama Bin Laden*. London: Verso, 2005.

Lee, Jeffrey. *God's Wolf: The Life of the Most Notorious of All Crusaders: Reynald de Chatillon*. London: Atlantic Books, 2016.

Lyotard, Jean-François. *The Postmodern Condition: A Report on Knowledge*. Minneapolis: University of Minnesota Press, 1984.

Mazzetti, Mark, and Scott Shane. 'In Yemen Bomb Plot, 2 Darkly Historical Inside Jokes'. *The New York Times*, 2 November 2010. [Accessed 20 December 2018]. www.nytimes.com/2010/11/03/world/03terror.html.

McCants, William. 'ISIS Fantasies of an Apocalyptic Showdown in Northern Syria'. *Brookings* (blog), 3 October 2014. www.brookings.edu/blog/markaz/ 2014/10/03/isis-fantasies-of-an-apocalyptic-showdown-in-northern-syria/. [Accessed 20 January 2019].

———. *The ISIS Apocalypse: The History, Strategy, and Doomsday Vision of the Islamic State*. New York: St. Martin's Press, 2015.

Peters, Edward. 'Have Muslims in the Middle East Really Remembered the Pain of the Crusades for a Thousand Years?' *History News Network*, 3 May 2003. https://historynewsnetwork.org/article/1398. [Accessed 20 January 2019].

————. 'The Firanj Are Coming – Again'. *Foreign Policy Research Institute: E-Notes*, 10 December 2004. www.fpri.org/article/2004/12/the-firanj-are-coming-again/. [Accessed 20 January 2019].

Phillips, Jonathan. *Holy Warriors: A Modern History of the Crusades*. London: Vintage, 2010.

Qutb, Sayyid. *Milestones*. Damascus: Dar al-Ilm, 1964.

————. *Social Justice in Islam*. Trans. John B. Hardie and Algar Hamid. Oneonta, NY: Islamic Publications International, 1953.

Richards, Donald Sidney. *The Rare and Excellent History of Saladin or Al-Nawadir Al-Sultaniyya Wa'l-Mahasin Al-Yusufiyya by Baha' Al-Din Ibn Shaddad: Or Al-Nawadir … Ibn Shaddad*. Aldershot: Routledge, 2002.

Runciman, Steven. *A History of the Crusades: Volume II The Kingdom of Jerusalem and the Frankish East, 1100–1187*. Cambridge: Cambridge University Press, 1987.

Scheuer, Michael. *Imperial Hubris: Why the West Is Losing the War on Terror*. Washington, DC: Chris Lloyd [distributor], 2008.

————. *Osama Bin Laden*. New York: OUP, 2012.

Schmid, Alex Peter, and Janny de Graaf. *Violence as Communication: Insurgent Terrorism and the Western News Media*. London: Sage, 1982.

Tolan, John, Henry Laurens, Jane Marie Todd, and Gilles Veinstein. *Europe and the Islamic World: A History*. Princeton: Princeton University Press, 2013.

Waldman, Peter, and Hugh Pope. '"Crusade" Reference Reinforces Fears War on Terrorism Is Against Muslims'. *Wall Street Journal*, 21 September 2001. www.wsj.com/articles/SB1001020294332922160. [Accessed 20 January 2019].

Wiktorowicz, Quintan. 'A Genealogy of Radical Islam'. *Studies in Conflict & Terrorism* 28:2 (16 February 2005), pp. 75–97.

Wright, Lawrence. *The Looming Tower: Al-Qaeda and the Road to 9/11*. New York: Vintage Books, 2007.

2   *Los Caballeros Templarios de Michoacán*
Knights Templar identity as a tool for legitimisation and internal discipline

Phil James

Los Caballeros Templarios de Michoacán, or The Knights Templar of Michoacán (LCT), was a criminal organisation, ostensibly founded in the early months of 2011 and effectively defunct by mid-2015, which operated primarily in Michoacán State, Mexico. In this chapter, we explore this case of borrowed identity, using evidence drawn from LCT's own code of conduct, known as the *Código de Los Caballeros Templarios de Michoacán*, to demonstrate that far from adopting the identity of the medieval Templar Order in a superficial manner, LCT actually drew deeply and creatively upon some of its most distinctive characteristics. Often subtly modified to fit the needs of its leaders, these were then employed to both support and legitimise the organisation's efforts to supplant the Mexican state as the perceived legitimate authority within Michoacán and as a tool for exerting control over their subordinates.

The lifecycle of LCT

LCT had its roots in an earlier organisation, *La Familia Michoacana* (LFM), which first emerged as an independent force in 2006 under the command of Nazario Moreno González and José de Jesús Méndez Vargas, claiming to protect the state of Michoacán and its populace from domination and exploitation by outside forces, including the *Milenio Cartel*, headquartered in neighbouring Jalisco state, as well as Moreno González' and Méndez Vargas' former associates the *Cartel del Golfo* and its then paramilitary wing, *Los Zetas*.[1] LFM was able to establish its ascendancy within Michoacán and, despite an apparent growth in tensions between the two leaders, was able to maintain this position for several years.[2] Early in 2011, however, a message emanated from within LFM, abruptly declaring that the organisation intended to disband following the reported death of Moreno González in a shootout with government security forces.[3] His death was 'confirmed' both by sources within LFM and by the Mexican government, but his body was never produced; on the ground in Michoacán, his survival appears to have been something of an open secret.[4]

Shortly thereafter, LCT announced its inception through a series of *narcomantas*, banners hung from prominent locations such as bridges across Michoacán, claiming to be a new organisation which would take up the mantle of LFM as defenders of the region.[5] Servando Goméz Martínez, a former lieutenant within LFM, emerged as LCT's public face, although in reality he served as a proxy and chief lieutenant for Moreno González, who continued to lead from the shadows.[6] In the following months, LCT swiftly assumed control over a large proportion of LFM's former operations, as opposition led by Méndez Vargas, still operating under the old name, collapsed following his arrest in June 2011.[7]

Given the continuity in leadership between LFM and LCT, it should be evident that these events do not in truth mark the birth of a new organisation, but rather an internal coup by the Moreno González-Goméz Martínez faction within LFM against the adherents of Méndez Vargas. Whilst the former group seized upon the opportunity that this split provided in order to rebrand, the organisation functionally remained the same in its underlying structure.[8] This chapter uses the terms LFM and LCT when referring to the organisation specifically in the periods before or after the split with Méndez Vargas respectively; ultimately, however, the continuity between these two periods should be recognised, and as a result, the term LFM/LCT will also be used where trends stretch across the full life span of the organisation.

LCT was to remain the dominant criminal group in Michoacán until 2014, when the organisation began to collapse under a combination of external pressures. First, its control over territory was challenged by the emergence of *grupos de autodefensas*, self-defence groups formed of *michoacano* citizens disaffected with life under LCT domination.[9] Around the same time, security operations decapitated LCT's leadership. Moreno González was tracked down for a second time in March 2014 and killed in a shootout; photographs and fingerprint evidence were released this time, confirming his identity.[10] The February 2015 arrest of Goméz Martínez, who is understood to have assumed full control of LCT following the death of Moreno González, appears to have left the organisation fragmented, with no clear successor in place.[11] Nevertheless, some remnants have remained in operation, and the name has continued in use until at least as late as 2017.[12]

Previous research on organised crime in Michoacán

In recent years, there have been several studies produced either from within Michoacán itself or with the benefit of fieldwork performed in the region, which have offered a sophisticated insight into the phenomenon of organised crime within the state. In a 2013 article, Salvador Maldonado Aranda has documented the underlying conditions that have allowed organised crime organisations to embed themselves deeply within the social fabric of Michoacán. His work reveals how a series of major infrastructure projects in the early decades of *Partido Revolucionario Institucional* (PRI) rule (late 1940s to early 1980s), which aimed to stimulate the development of the economy of this previously isolated and impoverished region and promote its integration into Mexico's national economy, also had the unintended consequence of enabling an evolution of the drug trade in Michoacán; localised drug production operations, which had existed in the state since the nineteenth century, now developed into large-scale trafficking networks. The PRI regime initially opted to regulate rather than suppress this burgeoning illicit industry, opting to make strategic concessions to traffickers in an effort to limit the potential for drug-related violence.[13]

Maldonado Aranda highlights the importance of the mid- to late 1980s as a turning point. The PRI regime reversed its policies, withdrawing investment in rural regions such as Michoacán following a series of economic crises, whilst at the same time shifting its approach to drug enforcement towards the mass deployments of security forces. This approach, despite its apparent lack of success in suppressing organised crime, and despite the numerous accusations of brutality enacted against the populace of rural regions which have resulted, has been maintained more or less unchanged almost to the present day. The policies of the past 30 years have had several ill effects. Not only have they alienated *michoacanos* once again from the Mexican state, triggering the emergence of a widespread perception that it has abandoned and even persecuted them, they have also enabled drug-trafficking organisations to step into the vacuum of power and resources which the state has left behind, by turns infiltrating its weakened and underfunded institutions and challenging them for dominance.[14]

Jerjes Aguirre Ochoa and Hugo Herrera Torres have offered an assessment of LFM/LCT's own motivations for exploiting the institutional vacuum within Michoacán, concluding that the organisation had evolved beyond the drug-trafficking roots of organised crime in the region. Whilst trafficking remained a lucrative sideline activity, LFM/LCT strove first and foremost to provide a credible source of alternative governance within the state, cultivating a perception of its own legitimacy amongst the populace which would enable it to assume – and generate revenue from – a wide range of the functions, which should have been performed by the state, but which had been neglected by its lapsed or ineffectual institutions.[15] A non-exhaustive list of these functions might include offering (or rather, selling) protection to the community against both common criminals and other criminal organisations; regulating the activity of small-scale drug dealers; offering debt collection services to private citizens; providing conflict resolution services between different individuals, economic, or political groups; giving permission for festivals and religious events; and regulating both crop production and agricultural prices.[16]

Falko Ernst offers perhaps the most satisfying exploration of the factors that have led LFM/LCT to refocus their operations first and foremost within the local sphere and to compete for legitimacy with the Mexican state. He argues that the slow collapse of one-party PRI rule in the last decades of the twentieth century brought with it a fragmentation of what had amounted to a state-sponsored protection racket over drug trafficking, removing any recourse but violence as a means of conflict resolution between the now-liberated criminal actors competing for control. By 2006, drug-related violence appeared endemic, and newly elected President Felipe Calderón Hinojosa responded by initiating a new 'War on Drugs', which included the mass deployment of State security forces to Michoacán, amongst various other regions, with a focus on suppressing trafficking operations, as well as targeting high-level members of criminal groups.[17] With hindsight, Calderón Hinojosa's policy is widely accepted to have been a failure. The targeting of the leadership of large, relatively stable organisations has led not to their eradication but to their fragmentation, accompanied by a further intensification of competition and violence.[18] Whilst security operations have not been successful in suppressing trafficking, the pressure placed on such activities by security forces, as well as by the increased competition which Calderón Hinojosa's War on Drugs has generated, has been the driving force in the move by criminal organisations such as LFM/LCT to diversify their income-generating activities.[19] Ernst emphasises that the bulk of these activities take place locally, within the organisation's core operational territory, stating that 'the local has emerged as the new center stage for Mexican criminal organizations' modes of organizational survival, in that resources vital to this end are generated here'.[20]

Like Aguirre Ochoa and Herrera Torres, Ernst reaches the conclusion that LFM/LCT strived to secure a perception of its own 'organisational legitimacy' amongst the populace of Michoacán during its period of dominance, enabling it to act as a force of alternative governance in the state.[21] What truly sets Ernst's study apart, however, is the unprecedented insight which he is able to provide into the organisation's motivations for doing so. In the course of fieldwork performed in the region during 2011 and 2012, he was able to achieve a remarkable degree of access within the organisation, including securing interviews with both Nazario Moreno González and Servando Goméz Martínez. Where Aguirre Ochoa and Herrera Torres characterised LFM/LCT's push for legitimacy as essentially opportunistic, driven solely by the vacuum in proper authority within Michoacán and the natural desire of criminal organisations to exploit the openings which such a vacuum might provide, Ernst's interviews with leadership repeatedly revealed that they had concerns of a more existential nature. The pressures created by the 'War on Drugs' had left LFM/LCT so dependent on its ability to generate resources within Michoacán, and thus so dependent on securing the goodwill of its populace, that the organisation's survival was now bound up with securing a perception that its existence and the propagation of its activities represented, at a bare minimum, the 'least-bad' solution for social order within the state.[22] As Goméz Martínez encapsulated the problem, rather more pointedly, 'If I treat them [the populace] badly, they will put a bullet in me'.[23]

To this end, Ernst emphasises that what might be termed the 'regulatory' aspects of LFM/LCT's governance project were paired with a range of other activities aimed at the generation of the social capital necessary to maintain the requisite perception of legitimacy amongst the *michoacano* populace. These included the construction of schools, the provision of subsidised groceries and medical services, the co-financing of housing projects and the distribution of agricultural machinery.[24]

That LFM/LCT made serious efforts to position itself as a legitimate authority within Michoacán now appears beyond doubt. There is, however, one aspect of this process which has been almost entirely overlooked in these studies; the adoption, part way through it, of a new identity as Knights Templar. Ernst notes only that Moreno González and Gómez Martínez told him they had adopted the new name for 'reasons of distinction', and for his own part suggests no more than that the adoption of a name with a religious root might '[reflect] the local socio-cultural setting'.[25] Aguirre Ochoa and Herrera Torres make no mention of any possible connotations of the new name whatsoever. Maldonado Aranda has offered the most perceptive suggestion, noting, albeit only in passing, that the new identity was used by LCT to self-identify as a movement seeking to restore public safety and peace.[26]

The *Código de Los Caballeros Templarios de Michoacán*

Our most detailed insight into LFM/LCT's adoption of Templar identity comes in the form of a 26-page pamphlet almost certainly authored by Moreno González, widely acknowledged to have been the architect of the organisation's ideology, which was produced shortly following its (re)foundation in 2011.[27] This pamphlet contains a list of 53 rules to be followed by all LCT members, known collectively as the *Código de Los Caballeros Templarios de Michoacán* ('Code of the Knights Templar of Michoacán'), accompanied by the much shorter *Juramento Templario* ('Templar Oath') referenced in one of these rules.[28]

Moreno González likely first came to engage with Templar ideas through the memory of the medieval order retained within the traditions of freemasonry. There is evidence to suggest that he himself was a mason; Ernst reported having been informed of Moreno González' fascination with the secret society during a conversation with a high-ranking member of LCT.[29] The presence of masonic symbols found syncretised with the Templar-influenced symbology of LCT in properties seized from the organisation by law-enforcement bodies would appear to strengthen this assertion.[30]

In the construction of his organisation's new identity as Knights Templar, however, he appears to have moved beyond masonic tradition to engage directly with material relating to the medieval order. The structure of the *Código* suggests a familiarity with – and a conscious attempt at mimicry of – the Rule of Order of the Knights Templar, the list of precepts initially set down by Bernard of Clairvaux around 1129 that governed the behaviour of members of the medieval order.[31] As we shall address in more detail later, the Rule was not the only part of Bernard's corpus of writing relating to the Templar Order with which Moreno González engaged when producing the *Código*.

Whilst the text of the *Código* has been written so as to address LCT membership directly, giving the appearance of mirroring the purpose of the Templar Rule as an internal document of instruction, the manner of its publication makes clear that the intended audience for the *Código* was not solely internal. The text is interspersed on roughly every third page with a series of idealised images of the medieval Knights Templar, and the resulting pamphlet was mass produced and distributed widely by LCT amongst the populace of Michoacán.[32] The *Código* is instead best interpreted as having had a dual function: first to convey to LCT's membership the behaviours and values which the organisation's leadership expected and, in some instances, needed them to embody, at least publicly; and second to justify LCT's existence to the wider populace of Michoacán by presenting an image of the organisation which befitted its need to be seen as the 'least-bad' solution for the provision of social order in that state.[33]

The adoption of the specific identity of the Knights Templar had a far greater role in this process than merely providing the underlying structure for the *Código*. The main value of Templar identity to LCT's leadership can be found in its utility as a paradigm. It provided legitimacy both to the efforts of leadership to exert control over their members and to the organisation's interactions with wider *michoacano* society, by establishing and appealing to a historical precedent for them. The ways in which a medieval military order might serve as a paradigm for a modern criminal organisation are not immediately obvious; however, when one allows for a certain amount of flexibility and creativity on the part of LCT leadership, they in fact prove surprisingly numerous. The remainder of this chapter explore in detail four examples where LCT appropriated and reshaped characteristics closely associated with the medieval order in service of its own ends: silence, communal life, protection and, perhaps most surprisingly, the possession of a spiritual justification for its defining struggle.

Silence

Members of the Templar Order were expected to maintain the relatively standard commitment, found in many Christian monastic rites, to remain silent during particular periods of time during the day or during the performance of certain activities. This commitment is often, if somewhat erroneously given its partial nature, referred to as a 'vow of silence'.[34]

For LCT, the maintenance of silence primarily – although not exclusively, as we shall shortly touch upon – meant the maintenance of a culture in which the efforts of outsiders, including both security forces and rival criminal organisations, to infiltrate LCT territory and operations were met by stonewalling. Clause 7 of the *Código* announced that 'All Knights must respect the VOW OF SILENCE; it is absolutely prohibited to divulge our activities and secrets',[35] whilst Clause 47 laid out the severity of punishment which anyone who disregarded this 'vow' could expect, stating that 'When a Knight [...] violates the vow of silence of the Knights Templar of the State of Michoacán, he shall be punished with the death penalty'. Whilst the *Código* only ever explicitly extended this obligation to the organisation's own members, the decision to immediately follow Clause 47 with another which discussed the role claimed by LCT in the application of justice within Michoacán, and which mentioned that the organisation would only kill when 'sufficient reasons' existed, offered a thinly veiled threat that the same fate might befall any non-member who was found collaborating with the Mexican authorities. The conscious usage of 'vow of silence' in the *Código*, playing upon the term's particular monastic connotations, clearly denotes an effort by LCT leadership to legitimise this culture of silence which it sought to impose through the invention of, and appeal to, a worthy historical precedent.

Communal life

The Templar Order required its members to give up their individual property and wealth in order to live the cloistered, communal life common to many strands of Christian Monasticism.[36] In Clause 30 of the *Código*, LCT's leadership used the equivalent Spanish term, stating that 'All the Knights of the Order of the Knights Templar are obliged to lead a *vida en común*, sober and happy, maintaining a low profile so as to not attract attention'.

Precisely what *vida en común* meant to LCT leadership remains unclear. Two options appear possible, each turning on a different interpretation of the phrase. The first is that LCT leadership applied the term loosely, in order to create a double meaning. Aside from the monastic definition, *vida en común* could also, with a little finesse, be employed to mean something along the lines of 'life as part of the community' or 'ordinary life'. If this was indeed the intended meaning, then we find the adopted Templar identity being used in quite a broad sense, with this allusion to the simplicity and togetherness of monastic life serving to reinforce the message that LCT members must live simple, inconspicuous lifestyles, functioning as respectable members of society and avoiding lavish displays of wealth, in order to avoid drawing attention to their illicit activities.

Alternatively, it may be that the more precise monastic definition is what was actually intended, with LCT leadership making a connection specifically to the cloistered nature of monastic communities. Under its previous guise as LFM, the organisation had required its new recruits – many drawn from substance rehabilitation centres which the organisation operated – to undergo an intensive 6–8-week period of indoctrination, which apparently included periods of silent reflection in conscious imitation of monasticism, perhaps reflective of the development of a proto-Templar identity for the organisation even before the split with Méndez Vargas.[37] Ernst, in the course of his field-work, noted that these efforts, which he terms narco-social engineering, continued under the organisation's new name.[38] It is possible that the term *vida en común* referred instead to these periods of enforced sequestration, with the organisation's adoption of Templar identity providing a sharper, more refined justification for their existence. This second explanation admittedly requires some supposition. Ernst, who discussed LCT's indoctrination efforts in some detail with the organisation's leadership, gives no indication that he heard this term used in this or any other context.[39] In some ways though, it does fit the evidence rather neatly. It would, for example, explain the specific reference to sobriety in Clause 30, which otherwise seems somewhat out of place.

Protection

The Templar Order was in many ways defined by its protective role. It was originally formed with the purpose of protecting pilgrims on the dangerous roads between the Mediterranean coast and Jerusalem. As the order expanded, it quickly assumed several other roles which fall under the broad aegis of protection, including guarding the marching columns of crusader armies, and constructing and garrisoning fortifications along the frontiers of the Latin States of the Levant.[40]

In Clause 2 of the *Código*, LCT claimed to exist for a very similar purpose, declaring that it was founded 'with the principal mission of protecting the inhabitants and the sacred territory of [...] the State of Michoacán', picking up where LFM had left off. It is not difficult to see the sense of legitimacy which the adoption of Templar identity might convey upon such a claim. As important as the association with the traditional Templar role of protection was in providing a justification for LCT's existence however, the value of this particular parallel to the organisation did not end there. The successful establishment of a historical precedent for the organisation's claimed role of protector would also assist in creating an aura of legitimacy around one of the organisation's major revenue streams. The organisation had long sought to exploit the identity it claimed as a protector of Michoacán to underpin a large-scale protection racket in the state, extorting 'taxation' from individuals and businesses in return for 'protecting' their property or their family from harm.[41]

A spiritual justification for struggle

In his treatise *Liber ad milites templi de laude novae militae*, known in English as 'In Praise of the New Knighthood', written sometime between 1120 and 1136, Bernard of Clairvaux effectively blended together the previously separate professions of monk and knight in providing the theological justification for the existence of the Templar Order.[42] By giving up their secular lives and submitting themselves to the Order and its monastic precepts, the 'New Knighthood' of which Bernard wrote were able to perform their otherwise inherently sinful profession, fighting, in a manner which was spiritually justified, as they now did so in service to a higher calling.

From the LFM/LCT organisation's earliest days, it was noted for presenting its own self-proclaimed struggle to defend Michoacán in starkly religious terms. When LFM first announced its existence in 2006 by rolling the decapitated heads of five members of a rival organisation onto the dance floor of a nightclub in Morelia, the state capital of Michoacán, the grisly display was accompanied by a message, which proclaimed that the victims had been the recipients of 'divine justice'.[43]

The *Código* marked an attempt at the refinement of these earlier ideas. In fact, Moreno González appears to have sought to adopt Bernard's justifications for the existence of the Templar Order wholesale, superimposing them onto his own organisation's claim to possess divine sanction for its defining struggle and thereby seeking to establish a perception of the legitimacy of this claim, once again through an appeal to historical precedent. Clause 20 of the *Código* expressly drew a connection between serving the organisation and serving God, and this message was reinforced through the inclusion of two other clauses, 49 and 51, which focused specifically on the idea of fighting. The first of these stated, 'A Knights Templar of Michoacán is a crusader in every moment, being committed to a double fight: facing the temptations of flesh and blood, at the same time as facing the spiritual forces of heaven'.[44] The second declared that:

> Every Knight must advance without fear, not neglecting that which might happen to his left and his right, with a covered chest and a soul well-equipped with the Faith. Relying on these two protections, he will not fear men nor any demon.[45]

Both of these passages were lifted, almost word-for-word, from Bernard's treatise. As tantalising as these inclusions are, however, I would caution against developing this argument much further and suggesting that their inclusion resulted in the coherent and widespread adoption of the Templar understanding of spiritually sanctioned conflict amongst LCT's membership. From the evidence contained within the *Código* alone, it remains unclear how deeply even Moreno González immersed himself in this aspect of Templar ideology; his attempt at grafting these ideas onto his organisation does not display great sophistication or nuance. I am not aware that his ideas were fleshed out more fully elsewhere; even if they were, however, the ability and willingness of the rank-and-file of LCT to engage with the complexities of theological arguments such as this should be considered with a heavy dose of scepticism.[46] Even so, the idea that the leader of a criminal organisation would take even these nascent steps towards drawing such a connection should be deemed a remarkable development in and of itself.

Conclusion

Recent studies by Maldonado Aranda, Aguirre Ochoa and Herrera Torres, and Ernst have each contributed to the development of an understanding that LFM/LCT did not exist merely as a 'drug cartel', but rather as a multifaceted criminal organisation, the bulk of whose revenue-generating operations were carried out within its core operating territory of Michoacán. In order to secure its access to these locally generated resources, the organisation developed a coherent project of alternative governance, competing with the Mexican state to be perceived as the legitimate authority in the region. The work of Ernst, in particular, has demonstrated how the organisation's leadership had come to view the ability to establish a perception of legitimacy within Michoacán – to represent the 'least-bad' solution for social order in the state – as essential for its survival.

The reasons why the leadership chose to adopt a new identity as Knights Templar in the course of its efforts to establish both legitimacy and strong internal discipline have, however, been little examined to this point. Through an exploration of LCT's widely distributed code of conduct, the *Código de Los Caballeros Templarios de Michoacán*, I have sought to reveal the level of flexibility and creativity demonstrated by LCT leadership in their utilisation of their newly found identity. The 'vows' of monastic silence of the medieval Templars were twisted to justify LCT's enforcement of a culture of stonewalling outsiders; the idea of communal life was perhaps used to reinforce the message that the organisation's members must live a modest, community-focused lifestyle, or alternatively to provide an appropriately Templar veneer to LCT's methods of indoctrination; and the role of the Templars as protectors is repurposed to justify both LCT's existence and its control over a lucrative protection racket within Michoacán. There even appears to have been a rudimentary attempt to reuse the theological arguments that provided the Templars with a spiritual justification for fighting, marshalling these in service of LCT's own claims that its struggles to defend Michoacán from rival organisations and law-enforcement agencies were divinely sanctioned.

These examples do not mark the limit of LCT's exploitation of its medieval namesake. Other instances of such borrowing can be found in areas as diverse as obedience, discipline, care for the poor, internal conflict resolution and iconography. I hope they do at least suffice, however, to demonstrate the remarkable flexibility and vitality of Templar identity in the hands of Nazario Moreno González, and the part that this identity played in LCT's efforts to both control its membership and create a perception of its own legitimacy within Michoacán.

Notes

1 Salvador Maldonado Aranda, 'Stories of Drug Trafficking in Rural Mexico: Territories, Drugs and Cartels in Michoacán', *European Review of Latin American and Caribbean Studies* 94 (2013), pp. 58–9.
2 George W. Grayson, *La Familia Drug Cartel: Implications for U.S.-Mexican Security* (Carlisle, PA, 2010), p. 25.
3 Elyssa Pachico, 'Familia Michoacana is "Completely Dissolved"', *Insight Crime*, 25 January 2011, <https://www.insightcrime.org/news/analysis/familia-michoacana-is-completely-dissolved>, [accessed 7 October 2018].
4 Falko Ernst, *From Narcotrafficking to Alternative Governance: An Ethnographic Study of Los Caballeros Templarios and the Mutation of Organized Crime in Michoacán, Mexico*, PhD diss., University of Essex, 2015, pp. 194–5, 217–8.
5 Hannah Stone, 'New Cartel Announces Takeover from Familia Michoacana', *Insight Crime*, 14 March 2011, <https://insightcrime.org/news/analysis/new-cartel-announces-take-over-from-familia-michoacana>, [accessed 7 October 2018].
6 Ernst, *Narcotrafficking*, pp. 88–9.
7 Patrick Corcoran, 'Mexico Catches Leader of Familia Drug Gang', *Insight Crime*, 22 June 2011, <https://insightcrime.org/news/analysis/mexico-catches-leader-of-familia-drug-gang>, [accessed 7 October 2018].
8 LCT's leaders confirmed as much in interviews conducted by Falko Ernst. See Falko Ernst. 'Legitimacy Matters: Los Caballeros Templarios and the Mutation of Mexican Organized Crime', *Journal of Money Laundering Control* 18:2 (2015), p. 141.
9 Dudley Althaus, '"El Chayo" Dead but Knights Templar War with Vigilantes Rages On', *Insight Crime*, 11 March 2014, <https://insightcrime.org/news/analysis/el-chayo-dead-but-knights-templars-war-with-vigilante-militias-rages-on>, [accessed 7 October 2018].

10 Jeremy McDermott, 'Mythical Leader of Mexico Cartel Dead – For Sure This Time', *Insight Crime*, 10 March 2014, <https://insightcrime.org/news/analysis/mythical-leader-of-mexico-drug-cartel-dead-for-sure-this-time>, [accessed 7 October 2018].

11 Michael Lohmuller, '"La Tuta" Likely New Leader of Knights Templar After "El Chayo" Death', *Insight Crime*, 11 March 2014, <https://insightcrime.org/news/brief/la-tuta-likely-new-leader-of-knights-templar-following-el-chayo-death>, [accessed 7 October 2018]; Steven Dudley, 'Mexico Captures "La Tuta" but Michoacan Struggles On', *Insight Crime*, 27 February 2015, <https://insightcrime.org/news/analysis/mexico-captures-la-tuta-but-michoacan-struggles-on>, [accessed 7 October 2018].

12 Patrick Corcoran, 'Mexico's Michoacán a Tangle of Rivals', *Insight Crime*, 28 November 2017, <https://insightcrime.org/news/analysis/mexicos-michoacan-tangle-rivals>, [accessed 7 October 2018].

13 Maldonado Aranda, 'Stories', pp. 46–9.

14 Ibid., pp. 51–64.

15 Jerjes Aguirre Ochoa and Hugo Amador Herrera Torres, 'Institutional Weakness and Organized Crime in Mexico: The Case of Michoacán', *Trends in Organized Crime* 16:2 (2013), pp. 225–9.

16 Ibid., p. 225; Jerjes Aguirre Ochoa and Hugo Amador Herrera Torres, 'Municipal Weakness and Crime: The Case of Michoacán, Mexico', *Revista Quaestio Iuris* 8:2 (2015), p. 928.

17 Ernst, 'Legitimacy Matters', p. 139.

18 Ibid., pp. 139–40.

19 Ibid., p. 140.

20 Ibid.

21 Ibid., pp. 140–5.

22 LCT leadership repeatedly used the phrase *de lo peor le menos malo* ('of the worst, the least bad') in their conversations with Ernst. Ibid., p. 142.

23 Ibid., p. 143.

24 Ibid., p. 142.

25 Ibid.

26 Salvador Maldonado Aranda, '"You don't see any Violence Here but It Leads to Very Ugly Things": Forced Solidarity and Silent Violence in Michoacán, Mexico', *Dialectical Anthropology* 38:2 (2014), p. 165.

27 Ernst observed a perception amongst LCT members that Moreno González was responsible for the organisation's ideological output. See *Narcotrafficking*, p. 170.

28 All references to the *Código* in general, or to individual clauses, relate to my transcription with accompanying English translation available at <https://www.academia.edu/s/526e9799a2/codigo-de-los-caballeros-templarios-de-michoacan>, [accessed 5 December 2018]. The transcription has been drawn largely from a scan of the original *Código* available at: <http://tribalanalysiscenter.com/PDF-TAC/Codigo%20De%20Los%20Caballeros%20Templarios%20De%20Michoacan>, [accessed 5 October 2018]. However, this pdf is missing p. 13; as a result, it has been necessary to reassemble the contents of this page from YouTube videos that display the relevant text.

29 Ernst, *Narcotrafficking*, p. 171.

30 Maldonado Aranda, 'Forced Solidarity', p. 165.

31 Bernard's first iteration of the Templar Rule has been translated into English by Malcolm Barber and Keith Bate in *The Templars: Selected Sources*, (Manchester, 2002), pp. 31–54.

32 Ernst reports in *Narcotrafficking*, p. 141, that the Código was distributed 'in vast numbers to local civilians' and was handed to him personally by a member of LCT with an intimation to 'grab as many as you want'.

33 There is an understandable temptation to deny that the *Código* served any internal purpose whatsoever and to treat it solely as an act of propaganda. The range of news reports that have claimed the involvement of LFM/LCT members in activities that transgress the rules laid out in the *Código* might be held to lend weight to this view. I would argue instead that it should not be considered irreconcilable that a criminal organisation might make a genuine demand of its members to behave in one manner in public, and yet expect them to demonstrate different characteristics whilst pursuing the organisation's clandestine activities. There are, moreover, certain aspects of the content of the *Código* – for example, Clauses 44 and 45, which together discuss the precautions which an LCT member should take when moving and operating outside their usual zone of activity – that serve no obvious purpose as propaganda. Their inclusion in the *Código* makes little sense if the document lacked a genuine role in LCT's internal governance.

34 Barber and Bate, *Templars*, pp. 39, 49–50.

35 Their capitalisation.

36 Barber and Bate, *Templars*, pp. 39–40, 49.

37 Grayson, *La Familia*, pp. 37–8.

38 Ernst, *Narcotrafficking*, pp. 176–7.

39 The details of these discussions are recorded in *Narcotrafficking*, pp. 174–76.

40 Malcolm Barber, *The New Knighthood: A History of the Order of the Temple*, (Cambridge, 1994), pp. 3–6, 34–7, 66–7.

41 Ernst, *Narcotrafficking*, pp. 73–4, 134.

42 Barber, *New Knighthood*, pp. 43–4.

43 Grayson, *La Familia*, p. 1.

44 Cf. Bernard of Clairvaux, *In Praise of the New Knighthood*, Trans. Conrad Greenia, (Kalamazoo, MI, 2000), p. 33.

45 Cf. ibid., p. 34.

46 Ernst's interviews with even relatively senior figures within LCT suggest a lack of clarity about certain details of the organisation's official ideology. See *Narcotrafficking*, p. 170.

Bibliography

Primary

Althaus, Dudley. '"El Chayo" Dead but Knights Templar War with Vigilantes Rages On'. *Insight Crime*. 11 March 2014. https://insightcrime.org/news/analysis/el-chayo-dead-but-knights-templars-war-with-vigilante-militias-rages-on. [Accessed 7 October 2018].

Clairvaux, Bernard of. *In Praise of the New Knighthood.* Trans. Conrad Greenia. Kalamazoo, MI: Cistercian Publications, 2000.

Código de Los Caballeros Templarios de Michoacán. http://tribalanalysiscenter. com/PDF-TAC/Codigo%20De%20Los%20Caballeros%20Templarios%20 De%20Michoacan. [Accessed 7 October 2018].

Corcoran, Patrick. 'Mexico Catches Leader of Familia Drug Gang'. *Insight Crime.* 22 June 2011. https://insightcrime.org/news/analysis/mexico-catches-leader-of-familia-drug-gang. [Accessed 7 October 2018].

———. 'Mexico's Michoacán a Tangle of Rivals'. *Insight Crime.* 28 November 2017. https://insightcrime.org/news/analysis/mexicos-michoacan-tangle-rivals. [Accessed 7 October 2018].

Dudley, Steven. 'Mexico Captures "La Tuta" but Michoacan Struggles On'. *Insight Crime.* 27 February 2015. https://insightcrime.org/news/analysis/ mexico-captures-la-tuta-but-michoacan-struggles-on. [Accessed 7 October 2018].

Lohmuller, Michael. '"La Tuta" Likely New Leader of Knights Templar After "El Chayo" Death'. *Insight Crime.* 11 March 2014. https://insightcrime. org/news/brief/la-tuta-likely-new-leader-of-knights-templar-following-el-chayo-death. [Accessed 7 October 2018].

McDermott, Jeremy. 'Mythical Leader of Mexico Cartel Dead – For Sure This Time'. *Insight Crime.* 10 March 2014. https://insightcrime.org/news/ analysis/mythical-leader-of-mexico-drug-cartel-dead-for-sure-this-time. [Accessed 7 October 2018].

Pachico, Elyssa. 'Familia Michoacana is "Completely Dissolved"'. *Insight Crime.* 25 January 2011. www.insightcrime.org/news/analysis/familia-michoacana-is-completely-dissolved. [Accessed 7 October 2018].

Stone, Hannah. 'New Cartel Announces Takeover from Familia Michoacana'. *Insight Crime.* 14 March 2011. https://insightcrime.org/news/analysis/ new-cartel-announces-take-over-from-familia-michoacana. [Accessed 7 October 2018].

Secondary

Aguirre Ochoa, Jerjes, and Hugo Amador Herrera Torres. 'Institutional Weakness and Organized Crime in Mexico: The case of Michoacán'. *Trends in Organized Crime* 16:2 (2013), pp. 221–38.

———. 'Municipal Weakness and Crime: The Case of Michoacán, Mexico'. *Revista Quaestio Iuris* 8:2 (2015), pp. 920–32.

Barber, Malcolm. *The New Knighthood: A History of the Order of the Temple.* Cambridge: CUP, 1994.

Barber, Malcolm, and Keith Bate. Trans. *The Templars: Selected Sources.* Manchester: MUP, 2002.Ernst, Falko. *From Narcotrafficking to Alternative Governance: An Ethnographic Study of Los Caballeros Templarios and the Mutation of Organized Crime in Michoacán*, Mexico. PhD diss., University of Essex, 2015.

———. 'Legitimacy Matters: *Los Caballeros Templarios* and the Mutation of Mexican Organized Crime'. *Journal of Money Laundering Control* 18:2 (2015), pp. 137–52.

Grayson, George W. *La Familia Drug Cartel: Implications for U.S.-Mexican Security*. Carlisle, PA: Strategic Studies Institute, 2010.

Maldonado Aranda, Salvador. 'Stories of Drug Trafficking in Rural Mexico: Territories, Drugs and Cartels in Michoacán'. *European Review of Latin American and Caribbean Studies* 94 (2013), pp. 43–66.

———. '"You don't see any Violence Here but It Leads to Very Ugly Things": Forced Solidarity and Silent Violence in Michoacán, Mexico'. *Dialectical Anthropology* 38:2 (2014), pp. 153–71.

3 Medievalism, imagination and violence

The function and dysfunction of crusading rhetoric in the post-9/11 political world

Hilary Rhodes

Since the events of 11 September 2001, and the deployment of a political, social and cultural discourse around the 'War on Terror', perhaps no area of medieval studies has enjoyed more of a resurgence than crusade scholarship, attempting to connect this modern-day phenomenon with its historical iterations. The original crusades, a series of military engagements that took place largely in the Middle East and were sponsored by the Catholic Church and powerful European warrior princes, are generally held to have spanned the 200 years from 1095 to 1291 and laid the groundwork for a millennium of troubled relations between 'the West and the Rest': a supposedly incompatible frontier of competing cultures, embedded in a distinct values-hierarchy. In this model, whereas one (the West) is rational, secular, forward, progressive, tolerant, humane and civilised, the other (the Rest) is irrational, sectarian, backward, static, intolerant, inhumane and uncivilised. This problematic paradigm, articulated most influentially in Samuel Huntington's article 'The Clash of Civilizations?' has been central to U.S. foreign policy over decades.[1] The recent rise of ISIS has also featured a nearly ubiquitous characterisation of its actions as 'medieval,' 'barbaric' or otherwise synonymous with the 'stone age', with a strong implication that this sort of violence is unknown to the Western societies they are attacking. The role of an 'imagined medieval' in this conflict is thus paramount – and arguably dishonest.[2]

The paths to approaching and deconstructing these beliefs must situate themselves in a matrix of fundamental questions. To begin, I must place this chapter into conversation with its wider field of reference: not just crusade historians, but modern political analysts, sociologists, cultural studies, the virtual world and popular entertainment. As a piece of media purporting to be about a medieval historical event, but ultimately speaking to modern-day interpretations of religion, politics, violence, extremism and toleration, the 2005 Ridley Scott film *Kingdom of Heaven* is well-suited for this sort of interdisciplinary analysis. There was some critical attention paid to *Kingdom of Heaven* both before and relatively soon after the film's release, highlighting specific historical tropes or errors, its general loose regard for its subject material or the underlying stereotypes even in the relatively sympathetic portrayal of its Muslim characters.[3] But one of the key contentions of this chapter is that to merely critique individual inaccuracies is to risk missing the context in which they operate. We must consider *why* modern discourse has created such particular notions of the crusades, 'religious violence,' and the perennial appeal of an imagined Middle Ages, whether heroic or barbaric, in constructing national narratives and fundamental beliefs about Western society, especially vis-à-vis its enemies.[4]

In this vein, Robert Jewett and John Shelton Lawrence have investigated America's addiction to 'mythic politics', how this model is created and fed through entertainment and popular culture, and this phenomenon's historical roots in the Christian ideal of 'salvific violence'.[5] Moreover, their treatment of the relationship between religion and violence should be connected to the critiques of Talal Asad and William Cavanaugh, who question the insistence that 'religious' and 'secular' violence are discernible and separate.[6] In their framework, this is purely a rhetorical device used to maintain the clash of civilisations thesis, where 'religious' violence must always be inexplicable, irrational and simple 'evil', in contrast to the justifiable, rational and necessary nature of 'secular' violence.[7] David Barker, Jon Hurwitz and Traci Nelson have highlighted the 'messianic militarism' amongst the American right wing that uses a specific social construction of apocalyptic Christian theology, another crucial component of a crusading ideology.[8] Tal Dingott Alkopher has constructed a helpful framework for viewing the historical crusades as an act of 'socialpolitik', where the traditional arguments that they were conducted either solely for cynical economic gain and exploitation of non-Western peoples, or as a simple excess of religious zealotry, do not pass critical muster. Her thesis for the cultural contingency of the crusades as an event deeply influenced by their medieval context is, for the most part, convincing. However, Alkopher committed, in my view, a serious misstep when she claimed that 'the crusades were a *reasonable* and *normal* social and political reality in the Middle Ages but alien and unthinkable (for the most part) in modern times'.[9] Whilst it is an error to directly equivocate the medieval crusades and the modern 'War on Terror', it is no less a mistake to ignore, dismiss or downplay their long and damaging legacy in collective memory and real-world politics. Given the West's (especially the U.S.'s) own mythology about itself, particularly in its most crude and unabashed form under the Donald Trump administration, as a white or 'Christian nation' explicitly predicated on the exclusion of Muslims and other people of colour, it makes even less sense to pretend that the West is approaching its project of ideological and military violence from a disinterested, objective or rational/secularist perspective.

I do not have the space to demonstrate the entire history of the physical, sociopolitical, legal, economic, cultural and religious apparatus built to support the crusades, which did anything but cease its operation after the fall of the city of Acre to the Mamluk Turks in 1291. Crusading rhetoric turned from 'killing the pagans' to 'civilising the pagans', as the project was taken up by writers, scholars and policymakers at the inception of colonialism in the fifteenth century. This eventually resulted in the eighteenth-century Enlightenment and the development of 'reason' as something specific to Europe and European men, over and against the irrationality and backwardness of non-Western, non-Christians.[10] This provided a useful partition for disavowing the embarrassing heritage of the crusades and the Inquisition, the so-called stains on 'religious Christendom', from the new project of 'secular Europe'. But as colonialism reached its height in the nineteenth and early twentieth centuries, crusading imagery, metaphors and appeals enjoyed a considerable renaissance across Europe, presenting a broad canvas on which mythologised and romantic histories could be painted and nationalist narratives given stirring moral resonance. Moreover, despite the critiques of liberal scholars (themselves indebted to a troublesome intellectual paradigm), it had never been dislodged from the imagination of rulers and common people alike in the first place.[11]

The attacks of 11 September 2001, therefore, provided the opportunity for these ideals of violence to be deployed in openly and proudly anachronistic guises. I must also raise a note of caution about the common framing device of 'Islam and the West'; why are a world religion and a geographical hemisphere conceptualised as distinct entities and perpetual adversaries? The insistence on labelling one as religious and the other as secular and 'rational' functions as a contingency of the post-Enlightenment worldview where reason trumps religion by its very nature. By virtue of centring on a historical event, this mindset (and the attendant moral judgment) is also chronological. The West's enemies must still be 'medieval', whereas it has supposedly left a blinkered, feuding, unstable and zealot world long behind.[12]

This is indeed a key feature of a crusading hermeneutic: one position is boundlessly and unqualifiedly in the right, whereas the other is utterly and even demonically in the wrong. Compromise is neither acceptable nor desirable. We see it in the remarks of President George W. Bush after 9/11, declaring that 'pure evil' was responsible for the tragedy, and in those of militant Islamic clerics such as the late Anwar al-Awlaki, warning his Western-raised listeners that being both American and Muslim was completely and traitorously incompatible.[13] Indeed, Bush's explicit use of the word 'crusade' caused alarm across the European world familiar with its intellectual baggage[14] along with fears that he was playing into Osama bin Laden's desired image of the conflict, and he was quickly forced to recant. Tony Blair, then prime minister of Great Britain, offered a modified line: this was not a war between Christians and Muslims per se, but between 'civilised values' and 'fanaticism'.[15] But the real question is why Osama bin Laden should welcome and encourage the same language that his sworn enemies were employing against him. When asked in an October 2001 interview whether this was a 'clash of civilisations', and pointed to his repeated use of 'crusade' and 'crusader', he answered firmly in the affirmative.[16] As Geraldine Heng remarked, 'For mujahedin the instantaneity of past and present often lodges in a hyphenated term, the Möbius strip of Crusader-Zionist, in which something new – the post-World War II creation of Israel – folds seamlessly into intimate convergence with nine-hundred-year-old medieval phenomena'.[17]

Kingdom of Heaven and its critics

The responses to *Kingdom of Heaven* thus form an extremely fertile avenue of inquiry, as they stand at the intersection of a popular image of the crusades and its critical reception. The 2005 film, directed by Ridley Scott and starring Orlando Bloom as a heavily fictionalised version of the real-life crusader baron Balian of Ibelin, dramatises the struggle for the Holy Land in the twelfth century, featuring the battle of Hattin and recapture of Jerusalem in 1187 by the Kurdish sultan and Muslim champion Ṣalāḥ ad-Dīn Yūsuf ibn Ayyūb (known commonly in the West as Saladin). Renowned in his own day, admired and respected by crusading kings such as Richard the Lionheart, Saladin has in modern times acquired a particular status as a towering culture hero.[18] Middle Eastern leaders such as former Syrian resident Hafiz al-Asad and ousted Iraqi dictator Saddam Hussein constructed themselves as mythical Saladins, employing imagery and emotional appeal to capitalise on his political status as the man to reclaim the Holy Land from

Western invaders, and in 2010, Saladin became the star of a cartoon series produced by al-Jazeera Children's TV.[19] An online blog designed to guide individuals to Islam features a biography of Saladin for free download, noting, 'One may ask why the author preferred [him] over other figures. The answer is that Salah ad-Din's life is connected with the manifest victory and liberation of Jerusalem from Crusaders'.[20]

Played by Syrian actor Ghassan Massoud in *Kingdom of Heaven*, Saladin was depicted in essential fidelity to the historical figure's reported traits of justice, fairness and mercy, taking aback an establishment accustomed to the 'evil Muslim' serving as stock antagonist. Director Ridley Scott explicitly referred to President Bush's 'crusade' remark when explaining his decision,[21] and journalist Robert Fisk described watching the film in a Beirut cinema. According to Fisk, the Muslim audience very much enjoyed seeing a big-budget Hollywood block-buster do justice to one of their favoured heroes – especially a scene where Saladin, after the siege of Jerusalem, picks up a fallen Christian cross from the debris and places it respectfully back on an altar.

At this point [they] rose to their feet and clapped and shouted their appreciation. They loved that gesture of honour. They wanted Islam to be merciful as well as strong. And they roared their approval above the soundtrack of the film.[22]

This message that 'extremism sucks and everyone should get along', as humorously phrased by Muslim blogger Hamzah Moin, was generally well-regarded.[23] Muslim response, however, was far from universally positive. On a mainstream online forum, user Abu Abdallah complained that Saladin was overshadowed and undercut by the fiction-alised, gorgeous Balian, and that an 'accurate and responsible' film would have featured him as the hero instead. Abdallah also critiqued Scott for his overall treatment of religion:

Unfortunately, Saladin (ra) is portrayed more accurately than Balian. As an agnostic humanist, Balian somehow redeems the extremist Crusaders in the film by questioning religion and the inherent worth of Jerusalem. The crusades and modern conflicts of extremist Christians and Muslims represent a deviation from tradition, while authentic religion offers inspiration and a way to virtue for people of all faiths.

[...] 'Kingdom of Heaven' tries to rewrite history by giving the virtues of Saladin (ra) to a crusader. While diminishing the presence of the Muslim exemplar of mercy and goodness, Scott also denies Christian virtue by depicting Balian as a secular humanist who is able to act perfectly without God.[24]

In Abdallah's view, religion is a pure, ahistorical and universal force for good, whereas the muck of secular politics and worldly empire-building has harmfully co-opted it. It is noteworthy that his critiques harmonised in some degree with those from the Christian side, with complaints that the depiction of Christianity and Islam as essentially similar or as mere 'moral systems' cheapened their authenticity (especially threatening Christianity's privileged and 'true' position) and that

> We are not, as Kingdom of Heaven would have us believe, all one [...] The way to move forward with relations between religions [...] is not to eliminate both religions [...] but to recognize real differences and to coexist peacefully in spite of them.[25]

Whilst both these critiques are valid and important, calling on religious believers to acknowledge and respect their differences rather than attempting to assimilate or destroy them, they rest on a notion that religion itself is essentially innocent and that it exists apart from its social, cultural and political manifestations (and their attendant prejudices) in human society – a view that the secular historian must reject. The film also is most certainly guilty of the modern view, with roots in the eighteenth-century Enlightenment assessments of the crusades, that they were motivated by simplistic medieval religious bigotry. In Scott's telling, the Knights Templar are the irredeemably villainous and extremist antagonists, rather than either Christian or Muslim secular leaders.[26] Whilst this is a useful ideological tool to reinforce the 'myth of progress', it does not represent the complexity of the historical, legal, social, political and cultural apparatus that invented and sustained the medieval crusades.

The criticism of *Kingdom of Heaven* from the professional academy, aside from its fast-and-loose treatment of the actual characters, situations and conflicts, centred on the notion that this history is 'more dangerous' to get wrong and that its determination to stress interreligious (or irreligious) cooperation was problematic and anachronistic.[27] By far the most blunt critique came from the late Jonathan Riley-Smith, professor of ecclesiastical history at Cambridge University at the time and one of Britain's most respected crusade scholars. Speaking before the film had been shot or released, Riley-Smith fulminated,

It sounds absolute balls. It's rubbish. It's not historically accurate at all. They refer to [Sir Walter Scott's romantic nineteenth-century novel] *The Talisman*, which depicts the Muslims as sophisticated and civilised, and the Crusaders are all brutes and barbarians. It has nothing to do with reality. [...] There was never a confraternity of Muslims, Jews and Christians. That is utter nonsense.[28]

He went on to claim that any such depiction would 'fuel the Islamic fundamentalists' and was 'Osama bin Laden's version of the crusades'.[29] Whilst Riley-Smith was correct to highlight that the extent of interfaith cooperation and the depiction of genuinely religious crusaders as the film's villains were both exaggerated, one must wonder why he was so adamant that portraying Muslims as 'sophisticated and civilised' has 'nothing to do with reality' and that any hint of cooperation between the Abrahamic faiths in the Holy Land (or indeed, any suggestion that the crusaders might have been in the wrong) would serve bin Laden's purposes. More interesting, however, is the fact that *Kingdom of Heaven* has indeed become co-opted into the message of Islamic extremism – yet not exactly how Riley-Smith envisioned it.

Appropriating the crusades

Jarret Brachman and Alix Levine have explored the phenomenon of 'virtual terrorists', in which young, usually English-speaking, Western-raised Muslim men gather on Internet forums to exchange opinions on their favourite clerics, rant about the need to join the struggle against imperialist oppressors, and imaginatively construct their fantasy identities as jihadists through avatars, images, audio clips and videos.[30] Whilst these digital personas rarely translate into real-world action, the possibility of self-taught individuals carrying out attacks (such as the 2012 Boston Marathon and 2017 Manchester Arena bombings) was, curiously, to the concern of U.S. law enforcement and Osama bin Laden alike.[31] Still more curiously, *Kingdom of Heaven* experienced a particular popularity in enjoining these young men to do just that. Employing footage from the film, especially scenes featuring Saladin, they used Photoshop and YouTube to create videos, set to Arabic *nasheeds*, urging for holy war.[32]

The fact of these would-be jihadis happily accepting and valorising their representation in a Western blockbuster film, and then using it to condemn the West, is remarkable. In the comments on these videos, they earnestly embrace the fantasy. In a typical example, a poster with an artistic rendering of the film Saladin serving as his avatar wrote,

'Allahu Akbar!! I promise i want to be like a Salahuddin Al Ayubi Insyaallah!!' whilst another praised, 'May ALLAH (SWT) Bless the great warrior Salah al-Din al Ayyubi with Paradise for his actions to liberate Jerusalem; ameen. May ALLAH (SWT) Send someone like him to liberate Jersualem [sic] again; Ameen'.[33] Others view the Taliban and al-Qaeda as Saladin's modern-day successors, stress his identity as a Muslim over all national and ethnic differences, and offer political appeals for Palestine and the rise of a new leader comparable to this medieval hero. Clearly, the nearly millennium-old conflict of the crusades is not a distant or irrelevant concern, but the context in which, with the use of modern technology, the message is framed and given resonance. They are embracing *Kingdom of Heaven* and its visual motifs, whilst rejecting its message of ecumenical tolerance and secular humanism, precisely because that is how they understand the situation. Having identified themselves as soldiers of the faith who are fighting crusaders, it becomes a natural step to envision Saladin as their timeless champion. Even Ghassan Massoud, the actor charged with the titanic task of playing him on screen, viewed him as someone who, if alive today, would have stopped President Bush's 'stupid' incursions into the Middle East and been a promoter of the 'feeling of humanity' between people.[34]

Is this proof of the claim that depicting Muslims as sophisticated and civilised is at odds with the historical record, and a validation of the thesis that jihad is irrational and absurd religious violence? As will be apparent, that is not the case. Instead, the forum participants are 'playing' their identities as jihadis, indeed very much like an actor in a film, and doing so not least because the crusade mentality, dialogue and popular imagination is decidedly reciprocal. The 2008 election of Barack Obama to the U.S. presidency, amidst enduring conspiracy theories that he was a secret Muslim, provided his ideological foes a golden opportunity to capitalise on anti-Islamic prejudices born from 9/11, constructing Islamophobia as a key component of Tea Party politics and supposedly central to American identity – a project viewed very much by its adherents as a crusade.[35] Nor was this an accidentally or arbitrarily chosen political strategy. 'Messianic militarism', using a specific social construction of apocalyptic Christian theology, is deeply embedded in the American right wing, central to the ways in which they frame their narratives and fight their battles.[36] As one of America's most cherished pieces of cultural mythology is that it is a 'Christian country', founded on 'Christian values', it becomes increasingly impossible to assert that the West's own violence is the justified fruit of secular, enlightened, non-religious (and thereby 'rational') roots. In short, the West has taken all the 'good' religion for itself and heaped the 'bad' onto Muslims. Likewise, violence and ideology opposed to that of the West becomes labelled 'medieval', whilst all rational governance is 'modern'.[37]

The unique American relationship to power, religion and violence is buttressed by a narrative of perpetual innocence. In this framework, America – the global commercial and capitalist empire, the richest and most powerful country on earth with the most military and technological superiority – is never the aggressor, but a passive and helpless victim unjustly attacked by simply 'evil' people who hate or are jealous of its freedom, opportunity and diversity. On a whole, the ambivalent or negative reaction to *Kingdom of Heaven* amongst the Western establishment is as easy to understand as the general Muslim embrace of its heroic Saladin: the film was holding up a mirror that the West found existentially uncomfortable to look into, bridging past and present and challenging the deeply rooted narrative of 'our' and 'their' violence. The election of Donald Trump on an unabashed racist, populist and nationalist platform has proven that, to the great dismay of liberal academia, the simplest conceptions of us-and-them identity politics still hold considerable and damaging sway.

Conclusion

Overall, a challenging portrait emerges. As I have contended throughout, *Kingdom of Heaven* is a film about the West's ideas of the crusades, and its condemnation of 'religious violence' from whatever perpetrator, structuring a classically liberal argument wherein peace can be achieved if religious individuals and organisations would just 'learn to get along'. Ridley Scott's subsequent work demonstrated that he still had this approach in mind. His 2010 film *Robin Hood,* starring Russell Crowe, featured a scene in which the protagonist confronts Richard the Lionheart for his controversial order to kill his Muslim prisoners in August 1191 during the Third Crusade, after the Muslim leadership had repeatedly broken or ignored the terms under which the hostages had been handed over. In this imagined scenario, a common man-at-arms not only directly challenges the king, but views his actions as a black mark on the crusade itself, an excess of pure religious bigotry with no possible explanation or justification. Whilst that may certainly be a modern perspective, it is by no means representative of the historical context in which the action took place (one which the Muslims themselves did not view as any final ultimatum, seeing as they were once more negotiating with Richard a month later).[38]

In Scott's well-meant attempts to critique a modern-day invasion and occupation of the Middle East, he made no attempt to question the ultimate paradigm that stigmatised 'religious' violence, understand the complexity of the crusades, or the mutual nature of crusading mentalities, imagery and invention.

Once more, my interest is not in petty fact-checking or poking holes in historical fiction intended to create a compelling story and to resonate with paying cinema-goers; indeed, I have argued that to do this is largely to miss the point. I do not care about *Kingdom of Heaven* or *Robin Hood's* overall accuracy; I care about *why* these storytelling choices are made, what mind-sets they are illustrating, what it tells us about how we view both the medieval crusades and the modern-day 'War on Terror' alike, and how collective memories have been preserved and deployed to make such a comparison still sensitive and relevant. Whilst modern scholars may wish they had the luxury of being the privileged interpreters of this legacy, and to do it solely within the bounds of traditional academia, it is impossible. The crusades have been reinvented down the centuries for countless purposes, imaginations and sociopolitical projects, and this continues in the post-9/11 political world. To simply complain about historical inaccuracies, anachronistic ideologies or factual liberties is to risk missing the point of why they exist, and the context in which they function. Crusade historians need not undertake their work with one eye on the headlines, nor manipulate medieval events to suit modern agendas, but they must have an awareness of the discourse they are contributing to and the legacy in which they are operating, as well as an acknowledgement of its consequences. To do otherwise is irresponsible.[39]

Ultimately, what are we to conclude? As has been argued throughout, the crusades are a profoundly potent metaphor for both sides in terms of viewing and creating the current global conflict, and one with troubling and violent contemporary application. This extreme rhetoric is a path not to peace and prosperity, but an ever-deepening crisis; we urgently require new paradigms and new scholarship. It is not my intent to suggest that modern nation-states will stop looking out for their own interests or producing religious-cultural mythologies to sustain them or that an unfortunately deep-rooted tendency to bigotry, war, and violence will easily be overcome. In making use of videos, films, Internet articles, blogs and other virtual content, as well as traditional historical monographs and perspectives, I have examined the changing shape of crusading rhetoric in the digital age, popular entertainment, religious versus secular violence, the selective blind spots and mobilisation strategies of Islamic fundamentalists and American nationalists alike, and the complexity and concern of our response to it.

Notes

1 Samuel Huntington, 'The Clash of Civilizations?', *Foreign Affairs* 72 (1993), pp. 22–49.
2 See Akil Awan and A. Warren Dockter, 'ISIS and the Abuse of History', *History Today* 66 (2016), <https://web.archive.org/web/20190205101057/https://www.historytoday.com/akil-n-awan/isis-and-abuse-history>; John Terry, 'Why ISIS Isn't Medieval', *Slate*, 19 February 2015, <https://web.archive.org/web/20190205101248/https://slate.com/news-and-politics/2015/02/isis-isnt-medieval-its-revisionist-history-only-claims-to-be-rooted-in-early-arab-conquests.html>; Graeme Wood, 'What ISIS Really Wants', *The Atlantic*, March 2015, <https://web.archive.org/web/20190205101255/https://www.theatlantic.com/magazine/archive/2015/03/what-isis-really-wants/384980/>, [all accessed 5 February 2019].
3 For a selection of work on *Kingdom of Heaven*, see Richard Francaviglia, 'Crusaders and Saracens: The Persistence of Orientalism in Historically Themed Motion Pictures about the Middle East', in *Lights, Camera, History: Portraying the Past in Film*, eds. Richard Francaviglia and Jerry Rodnitzky (College Station, 2007), pp. 53–90; Nickolas Haydock and Edward L. Risden, eds., *Hollywood in the Holy Land: Essays on Film Depictions of the Crusades and Christian-Muslim Clashes* (Jefferson, NC, 2008); Arthur Lindley, 'Once, Present, and Future Kings: *Kingdom of Heaven* and the Multitemporality of Medieval Film', in *Race, Class and Gender in 'Medieval' Cinema*, eds. Lynn T. Ramey and Tison Pugh (Basingstoke, 2007), pp. 15–29.
4 E.g. Patrick Geary, *The Myth of Nations: The Medieval Origins of Europe* (Princeton, 2002); Robert J. W. Evans and Guy P. Marchal, eds., *The Uses of the Middle Ages in Modern European States: History, Nationhood and the Search for Origins* (Basingstoke, 2011).
5 Robert Jewett and John Shelton Lawrence, *Captain America and the Crusade Against Evil: The Dilemma of Zealous Nationalism* (Grand Rapids, MI, 2003).
6 Talal Asad, *On Suicide Bombing* (New York, 2007).
7 William Cavanaugh, 'Does Religion Cause Violence?', *Harvard Divinity School Bulletin* 35 (2007), <https://web.archive.org/web/20190205120217/https://bulletin.hds.harvard.edu/articles/springsummer2007/does-religion-cause-violence>, [accessed 5 February 2019]; William Cavanaugh, *The Myth of Religious Violence: Secular Ideology and the Roots of Modern Conflict* (Oxford, 2009).
8 David C. Barker, Jon Hurwitz, and Traci L. Nelson, 'Of Crusades and Culture Wars: "Messianic" Militarism and Political Conflict in the United States', *Journal of Politics* 70 (2008), pp. 307–22.
9 Tal Dingott Alkopher, 'The Social (and Religious) Meanings That Constitute War: The Crusades as Realpolitik vs. Socialpolitik', *International Studies Quarterly* 49 (2005), p. 733.

10 Anouar Majid, *Freedom and Orthodoxy: Islam and Difference in the Post-Andalusian Age* (Stanford, 2004), p. 211.

11 See Knobler, 'Holy Wars'; Siberry, *New Crusaders*.

12 See Bruce Holsinger, *Neomedievalism, Neoconservatism, and the War on Terror* (Chicago, 2007).

13 Anwar al-Awlaki, *Inspire* (Al-Malahem Media, 2010), p. 58.

14 Peter Ford, 'Europe Cringes at Bush 'Crusade' Against Terrorists', *The Christian Science Monitor*, 19 September 2001, <https://web.archive.org/web/20190205123855/https://www.csmonitor.com/2001/0919/p12s2-woeu.html>, [accessed 5 February 2019].

15 Ibid.

16 Bruce Lawrence ed., *Messages to the World: The Statements of Osama Bin Laden* (London, 2005), p. 124. See also 'Crusader Wars', bin Laden's statement of 3 November 2001, in the same volume, pp. 133–38.

17 Heng, 'Holy War Redux', p. 425.

18 Omar Sayfo, 'From Kurdish Sultan to Pan-Arab Champion and Muslim Hero: The Evolution of the Saladin Myth in Popular Arab Culture,' *The Journal of Popular Culture* 50 (2017), pp. 65–85.

19 Jonathan Phillips, 'The Call of the Crusades', *History Today* 59 (2009), <https://web.archive.org/web/20130326161039/http://www.historytoday.com:80/jonathan-phillips/call-crusades>, [accessed 5 February 2019].

20 Islam for Universe, 'Salah Ad-Din Al-Ayyubi: Hero of the Battle of Hattin & Liberator of Jerusalem from the Crusaders', 22 August 2011, <https://web.archive.org/web/20190205124951/https://islamtheonlytruereligion.wordpress.com/2011/08/22/salah-ad-din-al-ayyubi-hero-of-the-battle-of-hattin-liberator-of-jerusalem-from-the-crusaders/>, [accessed 5 February 2019].

21 Gloria Goodale, 'Finally, a film sheds Muslim stereotypes', *The Christian Science Monitor*, 2 May 2005, <https://web.archive.org/web/20190205150644/https://www.csmonitor.com/2005/0502/p12s01-almo.html>, [accessed 26 November 2018].

22 Robert Fisk, 'Kingdom of Heaven: Why Ridley Scott's Story of the Crusades Struck Such a Chord in a Lebanese Cinema', *The Independent*, 20 June 2005, <https://www.independent.co.uk/voices/commentators/fisk/why-ridley-scotts-story-of-the-crusades-struck-such-a-chord-in-a-lebanese-cinema-492957.html>, [accessed 2 September 2018].

23 Hamzah Moin, 'Kingdom of Heaven Review', *Maniac Muslim*, <https://web.archive.org/web/20180325233850/http://maniacmuslim.com:80/kingdom-of-heaven-review/>, [accessed 5 February 2019].

24 Abu Abdallah, 'Kingdom of Heaven Review: A Muslim Critique of Kingdom of Heaven', *Sunni Forum*, 28 May 2005, <https://web.archive.org/web/20131107172632/http://www.sunniforum.com/forum/showthread.php?6095-Kingdom-of-Heaven-Review>, [accessed 11 October 2016].

25 Chris Neuendorf, 'Ridley Scott Epic Kingdom of Heaven Harmful to Christian-Muslim Relations', *Chains of the Constitution*, 2005, <http://www.neusysinc.com/columnarchive/colm0227.html>, [accessed 11 October 2016].

26 This includes presenting Guy de Lusignan, the disliked and controversial king of Jerusalem, as a Templar, which is inaccurate but represents a concerted effort to place all 'villainous' crusaders under the same banner.

The 'bad Templar' trope arguably began with Sir Walter Scott's 1825 novel *The Talisman*.

27 Goodale, 'Muslim stereotypes'.

28 Jonathan Riley-Smith, quoted in Charlotte Edwardes, 'Ridley Scott's New Crusades film "Panders to Osama bin Laden"', *The Daily Telegraph*, 18 January 2004, <https://web.archive.org/web/20190205145607/ https://www.telegraph.co.uk/news/worldnews/northamerica/usa/1452000/ Ridley-Scotts-new-Crusades-film-panders-to-Osama-bin-Laden.html>, [accessed 5 February 2019].

29 Ibid.

30 Jarret M. Brachman and Alix N. Levine, 'You Too Can Be Awlaki!', *The Fletcher Forum of World Affairs* 35 (2011), pp. 25–46.

31 Documents recovered from bin Laden's compound in Abbottabad, Pakistan, following his 2011 assassination by U.S. Navy SEALs, revealed the al-Qaeda leader's dislike of populist jihadis such as Awlaki and Faisal Shahzad. See Nelly Lahoud et al., 'Letters from Abbottabad: Bin Ladin Sidelined?', *Combating Terrorism Center at West Point*, 3 May 2012, p. 52, <https://ctc.usma.edu/letters-from-abbottabad-bin-ladin-sidelined>, accessed 26 November 2018].

32 E.g., 'Crusade Nasheed', *YouTube*, <http://www.youtube.com/watch?v=Pqk1Z-COR-90>, [accessed 11 October 2016]; 'arabic nasheed kingdom of heaven ضوخنس انكراعم مهمٔ', *YouTube*, [no longer available]; 'Salahuddin Nasheed', *YouTube*, 4 February 2010, <http://www.youtube.com/watch?v=qMNhEU-KoNbI>, [accessed 11 October 2016].

33 Spellings original. 'Akmal Danial' and 'Imperial Kaiserk' comments on 'Salahuddin Nasheed'.

34 Ghassan Massoud, quoted in Fisk, 'Kingdom of Heaven'.

35 Max Blumenthal, 'A Nation against Islam: America's New Crusade', *Open Democracy*, 13 January 2011, <http://www.opendemocracy.net/ max-blumenthal/nation-against-islam-americas-new-crusade>, [accessed 2 September 2018]. See also Abdus Sattar Ghazali, 'American Muslims Ten Years After 9/11', *Counter Currents*, 6 September 2011, <http://www. countercurrents.org/ghazali060911.htm>, [accessed 26 November 2018].

36 Barker et al., 'Of Crusades and Culture Wars'.

37 E.g., Gabriele, 'Debating the "Crusade"', pp. 73–92; Matthew Gabriele, 'Islamophobes Want To Recreate the Crusades, But They Don't Understand Them At All', *The Washington Post*, 6 June 2017, <https://www. washingtonpost.com/posteverything/wp/2017/06/06/islamophobes-want-to-recreate-the-crusades-but-they-dont-understand-them-at-all/?noredirect=on&utm_term=.7f362504952b>, [accessed 26 November 2018]. See also discussions in Andrew B.R. Elliott, *Medievalism, Politics and Mass Media: Appropriating the Middle Ages in the Twenty-First Century* (D.S. Brewer, 2017).

38 Thomas Asbridge, 'Talking to the Enemy: The Role and Purpose of Negotiations between Saladin and Richard the Lionheart During the Third Crusade', *Journal of Medieval History* 39 (2013), pp. 275–96.

39 This is becoming a particular awareness for crusade scholars, with seminars such as 'Teaching the Crusades in an Era of White Nationalism', at the International Medieval Congress at the University of Leeds in 2018.

Bibliography

Primary

Abdallah, Abu. 'Kingdom of Heaven Review: A Muslim critique of Kingdom of Heaven'. *Sunni Forum.* 28 May 2005. https://web.archive.org/web/20131107172632/http://www.sunniforum.com/forum/showthread.php?6095-Kingdom-of-Heaven-Review. [Accessed 11 October 2016].

al-Awlaki, Anwar, *Inspire*. Al-Malahem Media, 2010.

'Arabic nasheed kingdom of heaven ضووخنس انكراعم مهعم'. *YouTube*. www.youtube.com/watch?v=hC5NPszeHxk. [Accessed 11 October 2016].

Blumenthal, Max. 'A Nation Against Islam: America's New Crusade'. *OpenDemocracy.* 13 January 2011. https://web.archive.org/web/20190205150530/https://www.opendemocracy.net/max-blumenthal/nation-against-islam-americas-new-crusade. [Accessed 5 February 2019].

'Crusade Nasheed'. *YouTube.* http://www.youtube.com/watch?v=Pqk1Z-COR-90. [Accessed 11 October 2016; no longer accessible].

Edwardes, Charlotte. 'Ridley Scott's New Crusades Film "Panders to Osama bin Laden"'. *The Daily Telegraph.* 18 January 2004. https://web.archive.org/web/20190205145607/https://www.telegraph.co.uk/news/worldnews/northamerica/usa/1452000/Ridley-Scotts-new-Crusades-film-panders-to-Osama-bin-Laden.html. [Accessed 5 February 2019].

Ford, Peter. 'Europe cringes at Bush 'crusade' against terrorists'. *The Christian Science Monitor.* 19 September 2001. https://web.archive.org/web/20190205123855/https://www.csmonitor.com/2001/0919/p12s2-woeu.html. [Accessed 5 February 2019].

Goodale, Gloria. 'Finally, a film sheds Muslim stereotypes'. *Christian Science Monitor.* 2 May 2005. https://web.archive.org/web/20190205150644/https://www.csmonitor.com/2005/0502/p12s01-almo.html. [Accessed 5 February 2019].

Huntington, Samuel. 'The Clash of Civilizations?', *Foreign Affairs* 72 (1993), pp. 22–49.

Islam for Universe. 'Salah Ad-Din Al-Ayyubi: Hero of the Battle of Hattin & Liberator of Jerusalem From the Crusaders'. 22 August 2011. https://web.archive.org/web/20190205124951/https://islamtheonlytruereligion.wordpress.com/2011/08/22/salah-ad-din-al-ayyubi-hero-of-the-battle-of-hattin-liberator-of-jerusalem-from-the-crusaders/. [Accessed 5 February 2019].

Lawrence, Bruce, ed. *Messages to the World: The Statements of Osama bin Laden.* London: Verso, 2005.

Moin, Hamzah. 'Kingdom of Heaven Review'. *Maniac Muslim.* https://web.archive.org/web/20180325233850/http://maniacmuslim.com:80/kingdom-of-heaven-review/. [Accessed 5 February 2019].

Neuendorf, Chris. 'Ridley Scott epic Kingdom of Heaven harmful to Christian-Muslim relations'. *Chains of the Constitution.* 2005. https://web.archive.org/web/20190205151353/http://www.neusysinc.com/columnarchive/colm0227.html. [Accessed 5 February 2019].

'Salahuddin Nasheed'. *YouTube.* 4 February 2010. www.youtube.com/watch?v=qMNhEUKoNbI. [Accessed 11 October 2016].

Secondary

Alkopher, Tal Dingott. 'The Social (and Religious) Meanings That Constitute War: The Crusades as Realpolitik vs. Socialpolitik'. *International Studies Quarterly* 49 (2005), pp. 715–37.

Asad, Talal. *On Suicide Bombing*. New York: Columbia University Press, 2007.

Asbridge, Thomas. 'Talking to the Enemy: The Role and Purpose of Negotiations between Saladin and Richard the Lionheart During the Third Crusade'. *Journal of Medieval History* 39 (2013), pp. 275–96.

Awan, Akil and A. Warren Dockter. 'ISIS and the Abuse of History'. *History Today* 66 (2016). https://web.archive.org/web/20190205101057/https://www.historytoday.com/akil-n-awan/isis-and-abuse-history. [Accessed 5 February 2019].

Barker, David C., Jon Hurwitz, and Traci L. Nelson. 'Of Crusades and Culture Wars: "Messianic" Militarism and Political Conflict in the United States'. *Journal of Politics* 70 (2008), pp. 307–22.

Brachman, Jarret M. and Alix N. Levine. 'You Too Can Be Awlaki!'. *The Fletcher Forum of World Affairs* 35 (2011), pp. 25–46.

Cavanaugh, William. 'Does Religion Cause Violence?'. *Harvard Divinity School Bulletin* 35 (2007). https://web.archive.org/web/20190205120217/https://bulletin.hds.harvard.edu/articles/springsummer2007/does-religion-cause-violence. [Accessed 5 February 2019].

———. *The Myth of Religious Violence: Secular Ideology and the Roots of Modern Conflict*. Oxford: OUP, 2009.

Elliott, Andrew B.R. *Medievalism, Politics and Mass Media: Appropriating the Middle Ages in the Twenty-First Century*. Cambridge: D.S. Brewer, 2017.

Evans, Robert J. W. and Guy P. Marchal, eds. *The Uses of the Middle Ages in Modern European States: History, Nationhood and the Search for Origins*. Basingstoke: Palgrave Macmillan, 2011.

Fisk, Robert. 'Kingdom of Heaven: Why Ridley Scott's Story of the Crusades Struck Such a Chord in a Lebanese Cinema'. *The Independent*. 20 June 2005. www.independent.co.uk/voices/commentators/fisk/why-ridley-scotts-story-of-the-crusades-struck-such-a-chord-in-a-lebanese-cinema-492957.html. [Accessed 2 September 2018].

Francaviglia, Richard. 'Crusaders and Saracens: The Persistence of Orientalism in Historically Themed Motion Pictures about the Middle East'. In *Lights, Camera, History: Portraying the Past in Film*, eds. Richard Francaviglia and Jerry Rodnitzky. College Station: Texas A&M University Press, 2007, pp. 53–90.

Gabriele, Matthew. 'Debating the "Crusade" in Contemporary America'. *The Mediaeval Journal* 6 (2016), pp. 73–92.

———. 'Islamophobes Want to Recreate the Crusades, But They Don't Understand Them At All'. *The Washington Post*. 6 June 2017. www.washingtonpost.com/posteverything/wp/2017/06/06/islamophobes-want-to-recreate-the-crusades-but-they-dont-understand-them-at-all/?-noredirect=on&utm_term=.7f362504952b. [Accessed 26 November 2018].

56 *Hilary Rhodes*

Geary, Patrick. *The Myth of Nations: The Medieval Origins of Europe.* Princeton: Princeton University Press, 2002.

Ghazali, Abdus Sattar. 'American Muslims Ten Years After 9/11'. *Counter Currents.* 6 September 2011. www.countercurrents.org/ghazali060911.htm. [Accessed 26 November 2018].

Haydock, Nickolas, and Edward L. Risden, eds. *Hollywood in the Holy Land: Essays on Film Depictions of the Crusades and Christian-Muslim Clashes.* Jefferson, NC: McFarland, 2008.

Heng, Geraldine. 'Holy War Redux: The Crusades, Futures of the Past, and Strategic Logic in the "Clash" of Religions'. *PMLA* 126 (2011), pp. 422–31.

Holsinger, Bruce. *Neomedievalism, Neoconservatism, and the War on Terror.* Chicago: Prickly Paradigm, 2007.

Jewett, Robert, and John Shelton Lawrence. *Captain America and the Crusade against Evil: The Dilemma of Zealous Nationalism.* Grand Rapids, MI: William B. Eerdmans Publishing Company, 2003.

Knobler, Adam. 'Holy Wars, Empires, and the Portability of the Past: The Modern Uses of Medieval Crusades'. *Society for Comparative Studies of Religion and History* 48 (2006), pp. 293–325.

Lahoud, Nelly et al. 'Letters from Abbottabad: Bin Ladin Sidelined?'. *Combating Terrorism Center at West Point.* 3 May 2012. https://ctc.usma.edu/letters-from-abbottabad-bin-ladin-sidelined. [Accessed 26 November 2018].

Lindley, Arthur. 'Once, Present, and Future Kings: *Kingdom of Heaven* and the Multitemporality of Medieval Film'. In *Race, Class and Gender in 'Medieval' Cinema*, eds. Lynn T. Ramey and Tison Pugh. Basingstoke: Palgrave Macmillan, 2007, pp. 15–29.

Majid, Anouar. *Freedom and Orthodoxy: Islam and Difference in the Post-Andalusian Age.* Stanford: Stanford University Press, 2004.

Phillips, Jonathan, 'The Call of the Crusades'. *History Today* 59 (2009). https://web.archive.org/web/20130326161039/http://www.historytoday.com:80/jonathan-phillips/call-crusades. [Accessed 5 February 2019].

Sayfo, Omar. 'From Kurdish Sultan to Pan-Arab Champion and Muslim Hero: The Evolution of the Saladin Myth in Popular Arab Culture'. *The Journal of Popular Culture* 50 (2017), pp. 65–85.

Siberry, Elizabeth. *The New Crusaders: Images of the Crusaders in the 19th and Early 20th Centuries.* Farnham: Ashgate, 2000.

Terry, John. 'Why ISIS Isn't Medieval'. *Slate.* 19 February 2015. https://web.archive.org/web/20190205101248/https://slate.com/news-and-politics/2015/02/isis-isnt-medieval-its-revisionist-history-only-claims-to-be-rooted-in-early-arab-conquests.html. [Accessed 5 February 2019].

Wood, Graeme. 'What ISIS Really Wants'. *The Atlantic.* March 2015. https://web.archive.org/web/20190205101255/https://www.theatlantic.com/magazine/archive/2015/03/what-isis-really-wants/384980/. [Accessed 5 February 2019].

4   The *Reconquista* revisited

Mobilising medieval Iberian history in Spain, Portugal and beyond

Tiago João Queimada e Silva

The concept of *Reconquista* refers to an interpretation of history according to which the expansion of the Northern Iberian Christian kingdoms at the expense of Southern Iberian Muslim lands from the eight until the late fifteenth century was a long, concerted project of 'restoring' the old Visigothic and Catholic Spain after the 'illegitimate' occupation of the Peninsula by the 'Moors'. Al-Andalus is construed as an historical 'abnormality'; a hiatus in the history of Iberia, a territory that is seen as quintessentially unified and Catholic, were it not for the Umayyad invasion in 711.[1]

This teleological perspective was constructed and used during the Middle Ages, despite lacking the specific term '*Reconquista*', whose generalisation relates to the emergence of Spanish nationalism in the nineteenth century.[2] The idea was first advanced in ninth-century Asturian chronicles to legitimate the new-born Kingdom of Asturias-Leon, which claimed the legitimacy of the deceased Visigothic kingdom.[3] This myth would be a constant topic in Iberian historiography for centuries to come, especially in Castile-León. By the twelfth and thirteenth centuries, this perspective intertwined with the crusading ideal; the ideology of the crusade permeated Iberia and similarities were established between the anti-Islamic wars in Iberia and in the Near-East.[4]

This chapter deals with present-day uses of the medieval Iberian past for political purposes. I focus on the manipulation of the concept of *Reconquista* in far-right nationalist discourses. This inquiry draws on previous research by Martín Ríos Saloma and Alejandro García-Sanjuán. The former examined the origin and development of the concept of *Reconquista*,[5] whilst García-Sanjuán has focused on the survival of this concept in contemporary Spanish historiography, as well as on interpretations of the Andalusian past in contemporary academic discourses.[6]

Though lacking an in-depth examination on the use of medieval Iberian history in political discourses – such an analysis would necessarily require a *longue durée* inquiry upon some of the topics approached in this chapter – this essay contributes to the ongoing debate on the identity-building and present-day political uses of history, pinpointing some connections between the contemporary political situation and historical interpretation. The present chapter thus may be included in recent trends of research that focus on the phenomenon of 'political medievalism', i.e., the utilisation of medieval tropes in contemporary political programmes and debates.[7]

The recent emergence of far-right nationalism in several European countries has often been associated with the resuscitation of ultraconservative historical perspectives.[8] The rise of nationalism and xenophobia usually goes hand in hand with manipulation of the past in accordance with these political programmes. One of the main objects of manipulation in these discourses is Islam, which is presented as the archenemy of Europe.[9] The Iberian Peninsula is a *sui generis* case in this regard, since this region has a rich past of Islamic culture which Islamophobic nationalists have to deal with in their historical accounts.

Spain

The consolidation of the concept of *Reconquista* is connected with the emergence of Spanish National-Catholicism, an ideology that became hegemonic during Franco's dictatorship. The exaltation of the *Reconquista* was one of the building blocks for the construction of a Spanish national identity and was usually complemented by the denigration of the Peninsula's Islamic past. García-Sanjuán categorised the National-Catholic attitude towards al-Andalus as being of an exclusivist nature, since it excluded al-Andalus from the national history of Spain and denied it any positive role in the construction of Spanish national identity. Al-Andalus has merely a negative role in this process since, according to this view, Spanish identity is forged *against* al-Andalus.[10]

Even after the transition to liberal democracy in Spain in the late 1970s, there are professional historians who cling to the National-Catholic paradigm.[11] These historians provide far-right political programmes based on xenophobia and especially islamophobia with a degree of 'scientific authority'. Whilst García-Sanjuán dealt mostly with these tendencies in the academic world, I examine their persistence and adaptation in the political field. I first consider the use of the Iberian medieval past by Spanish nationalist movements.

The second of January, the date that marks the conquest of Granada in 1492, is a significant date for the utilisation of history to uphold Islamophobic discourses. Granada's municipality continues to commemorate the conquest of the last Muslim enclave in the Peninsula by the Catholic Monarchs Isabella I of Castile and Ferdinand II of Aragon. Every year, the event gathers supporters as wells as opponents of the commemoration. Those in favour are mostly far-right nationalist groups that take the opportunity to spread a National-Catholic historical perspective.

The Spanish party *Vox*, for example, used the date to connect the conquest of Granada to the 'greatness of Spain'.[12] The party claims to be proud of Spanish history and ashamed of those who 'reject' it. This Manichean logic – that contrasts 'true Spaniards' against 'false Spaniards' – recurrently appears in far-right discourse from several organisations.[13] The National Democracy party (*Democracia Nacional*, henceforth DN) also commemorates the conquest of Granada. The group defines the event as 'one of the greatest undertakings of history' and the Catholic Monarchs as 'the two most important figures of our history'.[14] DN's historical perspective encompasses all the commonplaces of National-Catholic rhetoric: it delineates a continuity of Spain as a nation back to the Romans and Visigoths, a quintessential unity that was broke by the Muslim invasion and restored eight centuries later by the Catholic Monarchs.[15] Al-Andalus, in turn, is described as a 'true hell' for Christians who remained in Islamic lands.[16] It is a teleological perspective of history, constructed around two of the main elements of DN's political discourse: hostility against Islam and cultural heterogeneity, on the one hand, and the safeguarding of Spain as a united nation, on the other. The *Reconquista* constitutes an argument not only against Islam and multiculturalism but also against those who defend regional autonomies and/or federalism within the Spanish state, as well as against peripheral nationalisms, such as the Catalan independence movement.

DN uses the *Reconquista* as an ideal for political mobilisation: calling for 'a new Reconquista', it explicitly establishes an analogy between the Umayyad invasion and present-day reality.[17] According to the DN, 'history is repeating itself', since the enemy within is 'opening the doors of Spain to the Muslim occupiers'.[18] Just as the Jews and a sector of the Visigoth elite are blamed for the success of the Umayyad conquest, also nowadays 'the elites of the country [...] behave like authentic traitors'.[19] An analogy is thus made between the Iberian Jews and Visigoth 'traitors' in 711, and the present-day sociopolitical agents who stand for a liberal and multicultural society. DN takes upon itself an analogous historical role as that of the Visigoth rebels led by Pelayo, the founder of the Asturian Kingdom who, according to the myth of the *Reconquista*, rebelled in Asturias in the aftermath of the Muslim invasion, initiating a historical process that would only end in 1492 in Granada. They thus claim to be treading in the footsteps of the Visigoth rebels, triggering a similar heroic feat as that of the *Reconquista*.[20]

For DN, Isabella and Ferdinand are precursors of many of the nationalists' policies: DN claims that 'the work of the Catholic Monarchs also had a profound social character', since Isabella allegedly 'elevated the standard of living of the Spanish people in a way never before accomplished' and persecuted bankers and usurers.[21] The culmination of the enterprise of the *Reconquista* is also seen as a precondition for Spain's imperial past, as it was after the conquest of Granada that 'Spain became one of humanity's greatest Empires, taking the light of justice, civilisation and hope to tens of peoples from all races and continents'.[22] The grandeur of Spain is, according to DN, being destroyed by contemporary politicians, who foment disunion amongst Spaniards, allowing separatist groups to operate, promoting immigration into Spain, allowing the 'Islamisation' of the country and granting the possibility for Sephardi Jews to acquire Spanish nationality. All of this 'with the clear intention of destroying the ethnic, cultural and religious homogeneity of the Spanish people'.[23] This analysis of the current political context motivates once again the use of the *Reconquista* for purposes of political mobilisation, as 'the time comes for a last crusade, of a new *Reconquista* to recover our future'.[24] The *Reconquista* is articulated here with the crusading ideal, which is in no way a new feature in Spanish nationalism, since the Francoist faction used crusading rhetoric to justify the rebellion against the Spanish Republic in 1936–39.[25]

Representatives of the traditional right-wing parties also convey National-Catholic interpretations of the Iberian past. On 2 January 2017, a politician from the Conservative *Partido Popular* (PP), Esperanza Aguirre, wrote a tweet celebrating the conquest of Granada as the forerunner of female emancipation in Spain, transforming the Catholic Monarchs into some sort of 'proto-feminists'.[26] Former Prime Minister José Maria Aznar, also from PP, gave a lecture at the University of Georgetown in September 2004, stating that Spain's conflict with al-Qaeda goes back to the 'Moorish' invasion in the eighth century.[27] The National-Catholic notion of the origin of Spanish nationality was even elevated to the status of programmatic policy for PP, as the party's sixteenth congress (June 2008) approved an amendment that located the roots of the 'Spanish nation' in Roman and Visigothic heritage, as well as in the political unity re-established by the union of the Castilian, Aragonese and Navarran kingdoms in the sixteenth century. Al-Andalus was completely excluded from their concept of Spanish national history and identity.[28]

The *Reconquista* is often portrayed by these groups as a common European enterprise, not exclusively Iberian. The *Falange Española de la JONS*, one of the several small organisations claiming the heritage of Primo de Rivera's Falange in the 1930s, defines Granada's conquest as 'the return of Spain to Europe'.[29] DN also refers to the conquest of Granada as a landmark in the defence of Spanish and European identities, invoked against those who work 'for the formation of multicultural societies that will end up turning us into a mere pile of unconnected people, without a common identity'.[30] For DN, the importance of the date encompasses the whole of Christendom, alongside the Battle of Poitiers in 732, the sieges of Vienna in 1529 and 1683, and the Battle of Lepanto in 1571.[31] Hostility towards Islam is presented by DN as a permanent feature of the history of Christianity, and the conquest of Granada is one of its most glorious episodes. Now, 'hundreds of thousands of Muslims again cross the frontiers of Europe', possibly bringing about 'the suicide of our civilisation', whose blame is to be put on multiculturalists.[32]

Another event that is laden with a heavy symbolic dimension is the Battle of Covadonga (722), the legendary victory of the Christians gathered around Pelayo in Asturias against the Umayyad invaders of the Peninsula. This event was first recorded in ninth-century Asturian chronicles and became a constant theme in medieval Iberian historiography.[33] According to the National-Catholic perspective, this battle is the founding event of the *Reconquista* and, therefore, sacred for Spanish nationalists. *Vox* even chose the Covadonga Sanctuary, a monument to the mythical battle, as the venue for the opening events of the campaigns for the Spanish general elections in 2015 and 2019.[34] The struggle against Islamic extremism was at the forefront of the event, together with restrictive measures against Muslim immigration into Europe.[35] The party's leader, Santiago Abascal, emphasised the 'liberty' of the Christian against the 'submission' of the Muslim, stressing in particular gender equality and the separation of Church and State, values that are presented as essentially Christian.[36] The anachronistic attribution of present-day liberal or progressive values to medieval Christianity appears to be recurrent in historiographical discourses from these political formations.

In 2019, Abascal again referred to the divine protection of the Covadonga sanctuary, this time explicitly establishing a nexus of causality between the Battle of Covadonga, the *Reconquista* and modern Spanish national unity and liberty.[37] *Vox* used the legend of Covadonga as a historical galvanizer for Spanish nationalism; a sentiment that the party attempted to mobilise and give political content, particularly in face of rising Catalan independentism. The Spanish 2019 general elections were a major success for *Vox*, as the party secured the entrance of 24 representatives into the Spanish Congress and raised its voting percentage from around 0.2 per cent (46,781 votes) in the 2016 general elections to 10.3 per cent (2,677,173 votes) in 2019.[38]

Spanish nationalists' views of the medieval Iberian past faithfully convey the National-Catholic narrative: Spain is viewed as an eternal – and, therefore, ahistorical – entity, whose Catholic essence was truncated by the Islamic invasion in 711. The fact that it was an invasion is stressed in order to delegitimise al-Andalus and portray the medieval Iberian Christian expansion in a teleological light; as Spain's 'manifest destiny', so to speak, or the 'return' of Spain to its Catholic roots and the annihilation of al-Andalus as some sort of 'historical anomaly'. This tradition has plenty of historiographical works to nourish it, since this discourse has recently been revived in several academic publications.[39]

The history of al-Andalus is useful for these far-right groupings to establish analogies that reinforce their political message. The Umayyad invasion is often compared to current Muslim immigration and radical far-right movements are compared to the small group of Christian resisters in the mountains of Asturias who initiated the long process of Christian expansion towards the south; Muslim immigrants are seen as religious fanatics that aim to impose an oppressive politico-religious system upon Christians who have lived in liberty up until now. Just as the Jews and corrupted sectors of the Visigothic elite opened the doors for the Muslims in the past, now we have 'traitors' and 'false Spaniards', who create the conditions for Europe's 'Islamisation' and the destruction of 'Western civilisation'.

Portugal

The conquest of Granada is also remembered by Portuguese nationalists, who equally see it as a European enterprise. The National Renovator Party (*Partido Nacional Renovador*, henceforth PNR) commemorated the military enterprise as 'the corollary of the great European and Iberian undertaking that was the Reconquista, large and long movement of resistance against the external enemy'.[40] For PNR, this enterprise not only gave rise to the Iberian nations, but its importance applies to all European nations, which, according to the party, are still under attack by foreign 'imperialisms'.[41] PNR claims that the remembrance of dates like these is increasingly relevant since 'we are being again invaded and we have to defend our culture and civilisation'.[42] As with Spanish nationalists, we encounter here a militant appropriation of the past, since history is used to draw analogies with the present which legitimise a given political programme. The remembrance of the past again serves as an element for political mobilisation.

When commemorating the conquest of Lisbon by the Portuguese King Afonso Henriques in 1147, PNR established comparisons between the present and the past: the 'Heroes' of the conquest of Lisbon were contraposed to current politicians and celebrities, examples of 'cowardice' and 'corruption'.[43] Whilst society at large choose the latter as their references, the nationalists preferred to revere the warriors of the medieval past, who were guided by values such as 'Honour and Sacrifice in benefit of our Land and People'.[44] PNR's concern with historical accuracy is scarce, since the party bases its praise of the 'heroes' of the conquest of Lisbon on the legend of Martim Moniz, an episode with no support in sources contemporary to the event.[45] Like their fellow Spaniards, Portuguese nationalists also make analogies between the medieval Muslim invasion of the Peninsula and present-day Muslim immigration.[46]

Another event that is celebrated by Portuguese nationalists is the date of the Battle of Ourique (1139), where, according to tradition, the founder of the Portuguese kingdom, Afonso Henriques, defeated five Muslim kings and was acclaimed as monarch. Contrary to their use of the conquest of Lisbon, here PNR questioned the historicity of the battle, reaching the conclusion that, despite the narrative's mythical elements, it was nonetheless one of the 'founding myths of the Fatherland' and it serves as a galvanising and exemplary event for current problems, i.e., the 'menace' of Islam to 'Western civilisation'.[47] Again, an analogy is made between medieval Christian-Islamic conflicts and present-day debates concerning Islam and immigration. PNR frames the Battle of Ourique in a universal conflict between Islam and 'the West'.[48] It is a perspective that resembles Huntington's famous (and much criticised) theory of the 'clash of civilisations',[49] but which has precedents in medieval Portuguese historiography.[50] This locates PNR within contemporary currents of Islamophobic thought that postulate the existence of a global war between 'the West' and Islam, a war that goes back to the very foundation of Islam and which continues today.

PNR follows its Spanish counterparts in conveying a historical perspective built upon exaltation of the *Reconquista* and denigration of al-Andalus. However, not all of the Portuguese far-right shares PNR's perspective: in the weekly newspaper *O Diabo*, connected with the Portuguese far-right, one notices that although some attention is given to the Battle of Ourique,[51] the main focus lies on past conflicts between Portugal and Castile-León,[52] the hegemonic Iberian kingdom throughout the Middle Ages. *O Diabo*'s preferred historical subject is the Portuguese expansion during the early modern age. The conquest of the North African city of Ceuta in 1415, which marks the beginning of the global European expansion of which Portugal and Spain were pioneers, takes a prominent position.[53]

The exaltation of Portugal's colonial past, instead of the *Reconquista*, points to a different sort of nationalism: contrary to the pan-European and racist tendencies of movements like PNR or DN, *O Diabo* appears to lean on a form of Portuguese nationalism based on the nostalgia for the colonial empire. This resembles more traditional forms of Portuguese nationalism that find their main politico-historical reference in Salazar's *Estado Novo* (1933–74). These different historical perspectives stem from the fact that PNR represents a more recent expression of far-right nationalism, a more European-minded and racist viewpoint,[54] whilst *O Diabo* draws from traditional Portuguese Salazarist nationalism based on the nostalgia of colonial possessions. Salazarist nationalism, although also ethnocentric and paternalistic towards colonised peoples,[55] was imbued with universalist and multicultural notions of the Portuguese nation.[56] Instead of focusing on the *Reconquista* as part of a universal conflict between 'European' or 'Western civilisation' and Islamic expansionism and religious oppression, its primary historical referents were the medieval struggles against Castilian hegemonic tendencies and Portuguese imperial expansion throughout the globe.

Occasionally, *O Diabo's* attitude towards Islam contrasts with that of PNR, such as when, for example, one of the newspaper's contributors, Pedro Soares Martinez, a law professor and a former minister of Salazar, appealed for the 'understanding between Christians and Islamists'.[57] The author mentions the incapacity of 'the so-called Westerners' to understand their 'Islamic brothers and their suffering', whilst pointing out Portugal's privileged position to foster understanding between these two worlds; due precisely to the country's Islamic past.[58] Martinez implies that the conflicts between Iberian Christians and Muslims are disproportionally remembered, in contrast with periods of peaceful coexistence, besides stressing the cultural and technical contributions that al-Andalus brought to the Peninsula. Martinez even proclaims that the Iberian culture is a product of Christian-Islamic confluence, asserting to be proud of that heritage.[59] This is an atypical argument even for traditional Salazarist nationalism, since the latter's discourse had in general a similar attitude towards the Muslim past as that of Spanish National-Catholicism.[60]

Europe

The use of the term *Reconquista* is not confined to the Iberian Peninsula, since it has spread to far-right circles on a pan-European level. The term is often used in non-Iberian political forums with the specific historical phenomenon of the Christian expansion over Islam in medieval Iberia going unmentioned. The word *Reconquista* (untranslated to 're-conquest') has entered far-right terminology in Europe divorced from the particular historical phenomenon to which it initially referred.

The Alliance for Peace and Freedom (APF), a grouping of several European far-right parties, published in 2016 a book entitled *Winds of Change – Notes for the Reconquista*.[61] In a congress of APF in Brno on 18 November 2017, Vice President Nick Griffin traced an apocalyptic scenario of present-day reality and delineated the following plan for the salvation of Europe: 'With the help of millions of white Western refugees whose children will help you get over your own demographic crisis, these are the nations that will lead first the resistance and then the long Reconquista'.[62] Griffin extrapolated the Iberian narrative of the *Reconquista* ('fall' of the Peninsula due to the Muslim conquest; long and gradual 'reconquest' of the territory) to contemporary Europe: the Afro-Islamic 'invasion' leads to the 'fall' of Europe, whose 'reconquest' is to be accomplished by the nationalists.

On 21–23 October 2016, Europa Terra Nostra, a foundation aligned with APF, organised an event in Germany under the title 'Freedom Congress' (*Freiheitlicher Kongress*). Its main theme was 'Reconquista or Doom', a formula that epitomises the contents of Griffin's speech in Brno.[63] Mentions of the *Reconquista* appear in many texts from APF, especially in the ones undersigned by Griffin.

Lastly, one must also mention how the term *Reconquista* has entered the far-right discourse in Ukraine: there is, for example, a blog aligned with the party National Corps with the title *Reconquista*, and whose motto is 'Today Ukraine, Tomorrow Rus' and the whole Europe'.[64]

The blog claims to represent 'an international movement of the Great European Reconquest based in Kyiv'.[65] Its political programme is based on the concept of *Intermarium*, a geopolitical project for a federation of states stretching from the Baltic to the Black Sea. This project was first developed during the 1920s in Poland but has recently been appropriated and adapted by the Ukrainian far-right.[66] This would be the first stage of a struggle which would culminate in the *Reconquista* of 'Paneuropa' from the clutches of 'neo-Bolshevik Russia' and 'multicultural EU'.[67] This demonstrates how the term *Reconquista* has ceased to be an ideological construction restricted to the Iberian Peninsula and has become a transcendental symbol for extremist nationalist movements all around Europe. It has become a mobilisational icon in the far-right's quixotic struggle for the 'reconquest' of the essence of an idealised Europe.

Conclusion

Spanish and Portuguese far-right nationalists are prone to establish analogies between the Iberian medieval past and contemporary realities, with the aim of legitimating their programmes historically. These ideological currents use the Iberian medieval past as a pivotal element in discourses of political mobilisation. They generalise and universalise the significance of specific medieval Iberian history. In doing so, the *Reconquista* ceases to be a particularly Iberian phenomenon and becomes a symbol of pan-European significance; a symbol of the necessary 'reconquest' of an imagined quintessential Europe from the hands of Muslim immigrants and liberals.

Beyond the 'Europeanisation' of the relevance of the Iberian *Reconquista*, these currents tend to use a discourse based on the dichotomy 'Us vs Them'; 'Us' being the nationalists, 'true Europeans', patriots etc.; and 'Them' being not only Muslims but also liberal and left-wing groups and individuals who reject the nationalists' xenophobic worldview. For the Spanish nationalists in particular, the *Reconquista* constitutes a historical argument against the present-day 'menaces' of Islam and multiculturalism, against regional autonomies and/or federalism inside the Spanish state, as well as against peripheral nationalisms, such as Catalan or Andalusian independence movements. The anachronistic attribution of contemporary democratic or progressive values to medieval Iberian Christianity, as opposed to 'Islamic oppression', is one of the features of much Islamophobic discourse that manipulates the Iberian medieval past.

Notes

1 Martín Ríos Saloma, *La Reconquista: Una Construcción Historiográfica (siglos XVI–XIX)* (Madrid, 2011); Martín Ríos Saloma, *La Reconquista en la Historiografía Española Contemporánea* (Mexico City/Madrid, 2013).

2 'Restoration' (*Restauración*) was usually the term used to refer to this historical process before the nineteenth century. See Ríos Saloma, *Una Construcción Historiográfica*.

3 Juan Gil Fernandez, ed., *Crónicas Asturianas*, Trans. Jose L. Moralejo, preliminary study by Juan L. Ruiz de la Peña (Oviedo, 1985); Kenneth Baxter Wolf, ed., *Conquerors and Chroniclers of Early Medieval Spain*, 2nd edn. (Liverpool, 2011).

4 Joseph O'Callaghan, *Reconquest and Crusade in Medieval Spain* (Philadelphia, 2003).

5 See note 1.

6 Alejandro García-Sanjuán, 'Al-Andalus en la historiografia del nacionalismo españolista (siglos XIX–XXI). Entre la Reconquista y la España musulmana', in *A 1300 años de la conquista de al-Andalus (711–2011): Historia, cultura y legado del Islam en la Península Ibérica*, eds. Diego Melo Carrasco and Francisco Vidal Castro (Coquimbo, 2012), pp. 65–104; Alejandro García-Sanjuán, *La conquista islámica de la peninsula ibérica y la tergiversación del pasado* (Madrid, 2013); Alejandro García-Sanjuán, 'La distorsión de al-Andalus en la memoria histórica española', *Intus-Legere Historia* 2:2 (2013), pp. 61–76; Alejandro García-Sanjuán, 'Al-Andalus en el nacionalcatolicismo español: la historiografia de época franquista (1939–1960)', in *El franquismo y la apropiación del pasado. El uso de la historia, de la arqueologia y de la historia del arte para la legitimación de la dictadura*, ed. Francisco J. Moreno Martín (Madrid, 2016), pp. 189–208; Alejandro García-Sanjuán, 'La persistencia del discurso nacionalcatólico sobre el Medievo peninsular en la historiografia española actual', *Historiografias* 12 (2016), pp. 132–53; Alejandro García-Sanjuán, 'Rejecting Al-Andalus, Exalting the Reconquista: Historical Memory in Contemporary Spain', *Journal of Medieval Iberian Studies* 10:1 (2018), pp. 127–45.

7 E.g. Wollenberg, 'New Knighthood'; Andrew B. R. Elliott, *Medievalism, Politics and Mass Media: Appropriating the Middle Ages in the Twenty-First Century* (Cambridge, 2017).

8 For an overview on the present-day European far-right, see Maik Fielitz and Laura Lotte Laloire, eds., *Trouble on the Far Right: Contemporary Right-Wing Strategies and Practices in Europe* (Bielefeld, 2016).

9 Emran Qureshi and Michael Sells, eds., *The New Crusades: Constructing the Muslim Enemy* (New York, 2003).

10 García-Sanjuán, 'Al-Andalus en la historiografia'. García-Sanjuán's research on nationalist interpretations of the Iberian medieval past, especially of al-Andalus, is restricted to Spain. We lack an analogous approach regarding Portuguese historiography.

11 García-Sanjuán, 'La persistencia'.

12 VoxEspaña, *Facebook*, 2 January 2018, <https://web.archive.org/web/20190 206105444/https://www.facebook.com/vox.espana/photos/a.467633 076675452/1299113786860706/?type=3&theater>, [accessed 6 February 2019].

13 Arlindo Manuel Caldeira, 'O Poder e a Memória. Heróis e Vilãos na Mitologia Nacionalista', *Penélope: revista de história e ciências sociais* 15 (1995), p. 132.

14 '2 de enero: 525 años de la Toma de Granada', DN, 2 January 2017, <http://democracianacional.org/dn/2-de-enero-525-anos-de-la-toma-de-granada/>, [accessed 21 September 2018].

15 Ibid.

16 Ibid.

17 Ibid.

18 Ibid.

19 Ibid. On the myth of the Jewish betrayal to the Visigoths by facilitating or provoking the Islamic conquest of the Iberian Peninsula, see Fernando Bravo López, 'La "traición de los judíos". La pervivencia de un mito antijudío medieval en la historiografía española', *Miscelánea de Estudios Árabes y Hebraicos* 63 (2014), pp. 27–56.

20 DN, '525 años'.

21 'Manifiesto del 2 de Enero', DN, 3 January 2016, <http://democracianacional.org/dn/toma-de-granada-2016/>, [accessed 15 May 2018].

22 Ibid.

23 Ibid.

24 Ibid.

25 William Viestenz, *By the Grace of God: Francoist Spain and the Sacred Roots of Political Imagination* (Toronto, 2014), p. 5.

26 Esperanza Aguirre (@EsperanzAguirre), Twitter, 2 January 2017, <https://web.archive.org/web/20190206111359/https://twitter.com/EsperanzAguirre/status/815942890857885696>, [accessed 6 February 2019].

27 'Aznar asegura en Washington que el problema de España con Al Qaeda "empieza en el siglo VIII"', *El Mundo*, 22 September 2004, <http://www.elmundo.es/elmundo/2004/09/22/espana/1095805990.html>, [accessed 15 May 2018]; García-Sanjuán, 'Al-Andalus en la historiografía', pp. 92–3. The use of medieval tropes in political and mediatic praxis is nothing new in the case of Aznar, since the Conservative politician dressed as El Cid in 1987 for an interview in the newspaper *El País Semanal*, when he was still the president of the Junta of Castile and León. Pablo Cantó, 'La mejor foto de Aznar no es la de las Azores: recuperamos su sesión como Cid Campeador', *El País Verne*, 7 April 2017, <https://web.archive.org/web/20190206111950/https://verne.elpais.com/verne/2017/04/07/articulo/1491558464_811336.html>, [accessed 6 February 2019]. I thank Sarah J. Pearce for calling attention to this point.

28 'Enmiendas a la Ponencia Política del XVI Congreso del Partido Popular', PP, 26 May 2008, <http://www.partidopopular.us/actividades/16congreso/enmienda_ponencia_politica_2.pdf>, [accessed 15 May 2018]; García-Sanjuán, 'Al-Andalus en la historiografía', p. 93.

29 Falange Española de la Jons Granada, 'Plan definitivo para el Dia de la Toma', *Facebook*, 31 December 2014, <https://web.archive.org/web/20190206110224/https://www.facebook.com/553396648025018/photos/a.553408244690525.1073741828.553396648025018/891325640898782/?type=3&theater>, [accessed 6 February 2019].

30 DN, 'Manifiesto'.

31 Ibid.

32 Ibid.
33 See note 3.
34 'Vox inicia su campaña electoral en Covadonga', *Europa Press Asturias*, 23 November 2015, <http://www.europapress.es/asturias/noticia-vox-inicia-campana-electoral-covadonga-20151123184927.html>, [accessed 15 May 2018]; Álvaro Carvajal, 'Éxtasis patriótico de Vox en Covadonga: "No vamos a pedir perdón por la historia ni los símbolos"', *El Mundo*, 12 April 2019, https://www.elmundo.es/espana/2019/04/12/5cb0b30921e-fa00e068b45e5.html, [accessed 16 May 2019].
35 'VOX inicia la conquista del Congreso desde Covadonga', *Intereconomia.com*, 20 November 2015, <https://intereconomia.com/economia/vox-inicia-conquista-congreso-covadonga-20151120-0000/>, [accessed 4 December 2018].
36 P. Martínez, 'Vox presenta en Covadonga su campaña y pide cerrar las mezquitas fundamentalistas', *La Nueva España*, 30 November 2015, <http://www.lne.es/asturias/2015/11/30/vox-presenta-covadonga-campana-pide/1848656.html>, [accessed 15 May 2018].
37 Carvajal, 'Éxtasis'.
38 'Resultados Elecciones Generales', *El País*, https://resultados.elpais.com/elecciones/generales.html, [accessed 16 May 2019].
39 E.g. Rafael Sánchez Saus, *Al-Andalus y la cruz. La invasion musulmana de Hispania* (Barcelona, 2016); Darío Fernández-Morera, *The Myth of the Andalusian Paradise: Muslims, Christians and Jews under Islamic Rule in Medieval Spain* (Wilmington, 2016). See García-Sanjuán's critique of some of these works in 'La persistencia', where he focuses particularly on Sánchez Saus' *Al-Andalus y la cruz*.
40 'Conquista de Granada lembra urgência de uma nova Reconquista', PNR, 2 January 2011, <http://www.pnr.pt/2011/01/2-de-janeiro-conquista-de-granada-lembra-urgencia-de-uma-nova-reconquista/>, [accessed 14 May 2018].
41 Ibid.
42 Ibid.
43 'Martim Moniz: um exemplo a não esquecer', PNR, July 2014, <http://www.pnr.pt/2014/07/martim-moniz-um-exemplo-nao-esquecer/>, [accessed 29 May 2018].
44 Ibid.
45 The legend of Martim Moniz – according to which this twelfth-century–Portuguese warrior heroically sacrificed his own life to permit the entrance of the Portuguese army in Lisbon during the conquest of the city in 1147 – has been widely spread in Portugal since the early modern age, although there are no sources contemporary to the conquest of Lisbon on which to base the episode's historicity. See Fernando Castelo-Branco, 'O Feito de Martim Moniz', *Revista Municipal* 84 (1960), pp. 5–18.
46 '21 de Outubro | Reconquista de Lisboa', PNR, 21 October 2014, <http://www.pnr.pt/2014/10/21-de-outubro-reconquista-de-lisboa/>, [accessed 29 May 2018].
47 '872 anos da Batalha de Ourique', PNR, 25 July 2011, <http://www.pnr.pt/2011/07/872-anos-da-batalha-de-ourique/>, [accessed 30 May 2018].
48 'Ourique: ontem, hoje e sempre!', PNR, July 2015, <http://www.pnr.pt/2015/07/ourique-ontem-hoje-sempre/>, [accessed 30 May 2018].

49   Samuel P. Huntington, *The Clash of Civilizations and the Remaking of World Order* (New York, 1996).

50   See, for instance, Tiago João Queimada e Silva, 'The Muslim *Archother* and the Royal *Other*: Aristocratic Notions of Otherness in Fourteenth-Century Portugal', submitted for publication in *Otherness in the Middle Ages*, eds. Hans-Werner Goetz and Ian N. Wood (Turnhout, forthcoming).

51   'Batalha de Ourique, alicerce de Portugal', *O Diabo*, 20 July 2015, <https://jornaldiabo.com/sociedade/batalha-ourique/>, [accessed 17 May 2018].

52   For example, the Battle of Aljubarrota (1385): '630 anos da Batalha de Aljubarrota', *O Diabo*, 10 August 2015, <https://jornaldiabo.com/nacional/630-anos-batalha-de-aljubarrota/>, [accessed 17 May 2018].

53   José Brandão Ferreira, 'A conquista de Ceuta: aspectos políticos e estratégicos', *O Diabo*, 17 August 2015, <https://jornaldiabo.com/nacional/conquista-ceuta/>, [accessed 16 May 2018]; Brandão Ferreira, 'Crónica de Ceuta 600 anos depois', *O Diabo*, 21 December 2015, <https://jornaldiabo.com/nacional/ceuta-600-anos-depois/>, [accessed 16 May 2018]; 'Os 600 Anos da conquista de Ceuta e outras datas com História', *O Diabo*, 6 December 2015,<https://jornaldiabo.com/cultura/datas-historia/>, [accessed 17 May 2018].

54   José Mourão da Costa, 'O Partido Nacional Renovador: a nova extrema-direita na democracia portuguesa', *Análise Social* 46 (2011), pp. 765–87.

55   Caldeira, 'Poder', pp. 132–3.

56   Caldeira defined traditional Salazarist nationalism as 'a nationalism [...] that [...] realises itself in its colonial dimension', ibid., p. 135.

57   Pedro Soares Martinez, 'Paz e respeito entre cristãos e islamistas', *O Diabo*, 28 December 2015, <https://jornaldiabo.com/sociedade/paz-respeito-soares-martinez/>, [accessed 15 May 2018].

58   Ibid.

59   Ibid.

60   Caldeira, 'Poder', pp. 132–3.

61   Stefan Jacobsson, 'New important book from the APF: Winds of Change – Notes for the Reconquista', APF, 7 December 2016, <https://apfeurope.com/2016/12/new-important-book-from-the-apf-winds-of-change-notes-for-the-reconquista/>, [accessed 16 August 2018].

62   Hynek Rint, 'APF Congress in Brno: Europe has to become a fortress', *APF*, 4 December 2017, <https://apfeurope.com/2017/12/apf-congress-in-brno-europe-has-to-become-a-fortress/>, [accessed 16 August 2018].

63   Nick Griffin, 'Report from the Freedom Congress in Germany', *APF*, 3 November 2017, <https://apfeurope.com/2016/11/report-from-the-freedom-congress-in-germany/>, [accessed 16 August 2018].

64   'Ukrainian ultras appeal to Polish comrades', *Reconquista Europe*, 8 May 2018, <https://web.archive.org/web/20180515230920/http://reconquista-europe.tumblr.com/>, [accessed 27 February 2019].

65   Quotation taken from Reconquista Europe's page in the social media platform VKontakte, <https://web.archive.org/web/20190206112945/https://vk.com/reconquista.europe>, [accessed 6 February 2019].

66   Mathew Kott, 'A far right hijack of Intermarium', *New Eastern Europe*, 26 May 2017, <http://neweasterneurope.eu/2017/05/26/a-far-right-hijack-of-intermarium/>, [accessed 18 August 2018].

67   'Reconquista Europe', *Vkontakte*; Kott, 'Hijack'.

Bibliography

Primary

Aguirre, Esperanza. Twitter, 2 January 2017. https://web.archive.org/web/2019
0206111359/https://twitter.com/EsperanzAguirre/status/81594289085788
5696. [Accessed 31 August 2018].

Cantó, Pablo. 'La mejor foto de Aznar no es la de las Azores: recuperamos
su sesión como Cid Campeador'. *El País Verne*, 7 April 2017. https://web.
archive.org/web/20190206111950/https://verne.elpais.com/verne/2017/04/07/
articulo/1491558464_811336.html. [Accessed 6 February 2019].

Carvajal, Álvaro. 'Éxtasis patriótico de Vox en Covadonga: "No vamos a
pedir perdón por la historia ni los símbolos"'. *El Mundo*. 12 April 2019.
https://www.elmundo.es/espana/2019/04/12/5cb0b30921efa00e068b45e5.
html. [Accessed 16 May 2019].

Democracia Nacional. 'Manifiesto del 2 de Enero'. 3 January 2016. http://
democracianacional.org/dn/toma-de-granada-2016/. [Accessed 15 May
2018].

———. '2 de enero: 525 años de la Toma de Granada'. 2 January 2017. http://
democracianacional.org/dn/2-de-enero-525-anos-de-la-toma-de-granada/.
[Accessed 15 May 2018].

Diabo, O. 'Batalha de Ourique, alicerce de Portugal'. 20 July 2015. https://
jornaldiabo.com/sociedade/batalha-ourique/. [Accessed 17 May 2018].

———. '630 anos da Batalha de Aljubarrota'. 10 August 2015. https://
jornaldiabo.com/nacional/630-anos-batalha-de-aljubarrota/. [Accessed
17 May 2018].

———. 'Os 600 Anos da conquista de Ceuta e outras datas com História'. 6
December 2015. https://jornaldiabo.com/cultura/datas-historia/. [Accessed
17 May 2018].

Europa Press Asturias. 'Vox inicia su campaña electoral en Covadonga'. 23
November 2015. www.europapress.es/asturias/noticia-vox-inicia-campana-
electoral-covadonga-20151123184927.html. [Accessed 15 May 2018].

Falange Española de la Jons Granada. 'Plan definitivo para el Dia de la
Toma'. *Facebook*, 31 December 2014. https://web.archive.org/web/2019020
6110224/https://www.facebook.com/553396648025018/photos/a.55340824
4690525.1073741828.553396648025018/891325640898782/?type=3&theater.
[Accessed 6 February 2019].

Ferreira, José Brandão. 'A conquista de Ceuta: aspectos políticos e estratégicos'. *O Diabo*, 17 August 2015. https://jornaldiabo.com/nacional/conquista-
ceuta/. [Accessed 16 May 2018].

———. 'Crónica de Ceuta 600 anos depois'. *O Diabo*, 21 December 2015.
https://jornaldiabo.com/nacional/ceuta-600-anos-depois/. [Accessed 16
May 2018].

Griffin, Nick. 'Report from the Freedom Congress in Germany'. *APF*, 3
November 2017. https://apfeurope.com/2016/11/report-from-the-freedom-
congress-in-germany/. [Accessed 16 August 2018].

Intereconomia.com. 'VOX inicia la conquista del Congreso desde Covadonga'. 20 November 2015. https://intereconomia.com/economia/vox-inicia-conquista-congreso-covadonga-20151120-0000/. [Accessed 16 May 2018].

Jacobsson, Stefan. 'New Important Book from the APF: Winds of Change – Notes for the Reconquista'. *APF*, 7 December 2016. https://apfeurope. com/2016/12/new-important-book-from-the-apf-winds-of-change-notes-for-the-reconquista/. [Accessed 16 August 2018].

Martínez, P. 'Vox presenta en Covadonga su campaña y pide cerrar las mezquitas fundamentalistas'. *La Nueva España*, 30 November 2015. www. lne.es/asturias/2015/11/30/vox-presenta-covadonga-campana-pide/1848656. html. [Accessed 15 May 2018].

Martinez, Pedro Soares. 'Paz e respeito entre cristãos e islamistas'. *O Diabo*, 28 December 2015. https://jornaldiabo.com/sociedade/paz-respeito-soares-martinez/. [Accessed 15 May 2018].

Mundo, El. 'Aznar asegura en Washington que el problema de España con Al Qaeda "empieza en el siglo VIII"'. 22 September 2004. www. elmundo.es/elmundo/2004/09/22/espana/1095805990.html. [Accessed 15 May 2018].

Partido Nacional Renovador. 'Conquista de Granada lembra urgência de uma nova Reconquista'. 2 January 2011. www.pnr.pt/2011/01/2-de-janeiro-conquista-de-granada-lembra-urgencia-de-uma-nova-reconquista/. [Accessed 14 May 2018].

———. '872 anos da Batalha de Ourique'. 25 July 2011. www.pnr.pt/2011/07/872-anos-da-batalha-de-ourique/. [Accessed 30 May 2018].

———. 'Martim Moniz: um exemplo a não esquecer'. July 2014. www.pnr. pt/2014/07/martim-moniz-um-exemplo-nao-esquecer/. [Accessed 29 May 2018].

———. '21 de Outubro | Reconquista de Lisboa'. 21 October 2014. www. pnr.pt/2014/10/21-de-outubro-reconquista-de-lisboa/. [Accessed 29 May 2018].

———. 'Ourique: ontem, hoje e sempre!' 25 July 2015. www.pnr.pt/2015/07/ourique-ontem-hoje-sempre/. [Accessed 30 May 2018].

Partido Popular. 'Enmiendas a la Ponencia Política del XVI Congreso del Partido Popular'. 26 May 2008. www.partidopopular.us/actividades/16congreso/enmienda_ponencia_politica_2.pdf. [Accessed 15 May 2018].

'Reconquista Europe'. *VKontakte*. https://web.archive.org/web/20190206112945/https://vk.com/reconquista.europe. [Accessed 6 February 2019].

'Resultados Elecciones Generales'. *El País*. https://resultados.elpais.com/elecciones/generales.html. [Accessed 16 May 2019].

Rint, Hynek. 'APF Congress in Brno: Europe has to become a Fortress'. *APF*, 4 December 2017. https://apfeurope.com/2017/12/apf-congress-in-brno-europe-has-to-become-a-fortress/. [Accessed 16 August 2018].

'Ukrainian ultras appeal to Polish comrades'. *Reconquista Europe*. 8 May 2018. https://web.archive.org/web/20180515230920/http://reconquista-europe. tumblr.com/. [Accessed 27 February 2019].

Vox España. Facebook, 2 January 2018. https://web.archive.org/web/2019020 6105444/https://www.facebook.com/vox.espana/photos/a.467633076675452/ 1299113786860706/?type=3&theater. [Accessed 6 February 2019].

Secondary

Bravo López, Fernando. 'La "traición de los judíos". La pervivencia de un mito antijudío medieval en la historiografía española'. *Miscelánea de Estudios Árabes y Hebraicos* 63 (2014), pp. 27–56.

Caldeira, Arlindo Manuel. 'O Poder e a Memória. Heróis e Vilãos na Mitologia Nacionalista'. *Penélope: revista de história e ciências sociais* 15 (1995), pp. 121–39.

Castelo-Branco, Fernando. 'O Feito de Martim Moniz'. *Revista Municipal* 84 (1960), pp. 5–18.

Costa, José Mourão da. 'O Partido Nacional Renovador: a nova extrema-direita na democracia portuguesa'. *Análise Social* 46 (2011), pp. 765–87.

Elliott, Andrew B. R. *Medievalism, Politics and Mass Media: Appropriating the Middle Ages in the Twenty-First Century*. Cambridge: D.S. Brewer, 2017.

Fernandez, Juan Gil, ed. *Crónicas Asturianas*. Trans. Jose L. Moralejo, preliminary study by Juan L. Ruiz de la Peña. Oviedo: Universidad de Oviedo, 1985.

Fernández-Morera, Darío. *The Myth of the Andalusian Paradise: Muslims, Christians and Jews Under Islamic Rule in Medieval Spain*. Wilmington: ISI Books, 2016.

Fielitz, Maik and Laura Lotte Laloire, eds. *Trouble on the Far Right: Contemporary Right-Wing Strategies and Practices in Europe*. Bielefeld: Transcript Verlag, 2016.

García-Sanjuán, Alejandro. 'Al-Andalus en la historiografía del nacionalismo españolista (siglos XIX–XXI). Entre la Reconquista y la España musulmana'. In *A 1300 años de la conquista de al-Andalus (711–2011): Historia, cultura y legado del Islam en la Península Ibérica*, eds. Diego Melo Carrasco and Francisco Vidal Castro. Coquimbo: Ediciones Altazor, 2012. pp. 65–104.

———. *La conquista islámica de la península ibérica y la tergiversación del pasado*. Madrid: Marcial Pons Historia, 2013.

———. 'La distorsión de al-Andalus en la memoria histórica española'. *Intus-Legere Historia* 2:2 (2013), pp. 61–76.

———. 'Al-Andalus en el nacionalcatolicismo español: la historiografía de época franquista (1939–1960)'. In *El franquismo y la apropiación del pasado. El uso de la historia, de la arqueologia y de la historia del arte para la legitimación de la dictadura*, ed. Francisco J. Moreno Martín. Madrid: Editorial Pablo Iglesias, 2016. pp. 189–208.

———. 'La persistencia del discurso nacionalcatólico sobre el Medievo peninsular en la historiografia española actual'. *Historiografías* 12 (2016), pp. 132–53.

————. 'Rejecting Al-Andalus, Exalting the Reconquista: Historical Memory in Contemporary Spain'. *Journal of Medieval Iberian Studies* 10:1 (2018), pp. 127–45.

Huntington, Samuel P. *The Clash of Civilizations and the Remaking of World Order*. New York: Simon & Schuster, 1996.

Kott, Mathew. 'A Far Right Hijack of Intermarium'. *New Eastern Europe*, 26 May 2017. http://neweasterneurope.eu/2017/05/26/a-far-right-hijack-of-intermarium/. [Accessed 18 August 2018].

O'Callaghan, Joseph F. *Reconquest and Crusade in Medieval Spain*. Philadelphia: University of Pennsylvania Press, 2003.

Qureshi, Emran and Michael Sells, eds. *The New Crusades: Constructing the Muslim Enemy*. New York: Columbia University Press, 2003.

Ríos Saloma, Martín. *La Reconquista: Una Construcción Historiográfica (siglos XVI–XIX)*. Madrid: Marcial Pons, 2011.

————. *La Reconquista en la Historiografía Española Contemporánea*. Mexico City/Madrid: Instituto de Investigaciones Históricas de la Universidad Autónoma de México/Ediciones Sílex, 2013.

Sánchez Saus, Rafael. *Al-Andalus y la cruz. La invasion musulmana de Hispania*. Barcelona: Stella Maris, 2016.

Silva, Tiago João Queimada e. 'The Muslim *Archother* and the Royal *Other*: Aristocratic Notions of Otherness in Fourteenth-Century Portugal'. Submitted for publication in *Otherness in the Middle Ages*, eds. Hans-Werner Goetz and Ian N. Wood. Turnhout: Brepols Publishers, forthcoming.

Viestenz, William. *By the Grace of God: Francoist Spain and the Sacred Roots of Political Imagination*. Toronto: University of Toronto Press, 2014.

Wolf, Kenneth Baxter, ed. *Conquerors and Chroniclers of Early Medieval Spain*. 2nd edn. Liverpool: Liverpool University Press, 2011.

Wollenberg, Daniel. 'The New Knighthood: Terrorism and the Medieval'. *Postmedieval* 5 (2014), pp. 21–33.

5 The reception of the crusades in the contemporary Catholic Church

'Purification of memory' or medieval nostalgia?

Marco Giardini

> The Crusades intended to liberate the Holy Land, and especially the Holy Sepulcher, from the hands of the infidels: without a doubt, a most elevated and noble goal! Besides, from a historical point of view, their purpose was to defend the faith and the civilization of the Christian West against Islam.[1]
>
> Pope Pius XII, 24 June 1944

> Let us ask pardon for the divisions which have occurred among Christians, for the violence some have used in the service of the truth and for the distrustful and hostile attitudes sometimes taken towards the followers of other religions.[2]
>
> Pope John Paul II, 12 March 2000

The above quotations could not be more divergent. They were issued by two popes: Pius XII, who, in the middle of the dramatic events that took place in Rome during the last years of Second World War, rekindled the religious zeal of a group of missionaries by comparing their efforts to the crusading endeavour, and John Paul II, during the famous 'plea for forgiveness' issued amidst the Great Jubilee of 2000, on the 'Day of Pardon'. Whilst the crusades were not explicitly mentioned in John Paul's statement, references to the crusades were frequent in numerous declarations that the Polish pope issued before 2000. In all of them, the holy wars of the past were understood as an example of anti-evangelical actions that required a special 'purification of memory'; an act that was considered unavoidable in order for the Church to pursue its evangelical and missionary task at the beginning of the new Millennium.[3]

How can we understand this striking opposition in evaluation of the crusades? Did the words of John Paul II obliterate the previous positive assessment of Pius XII? Or, are there still Catholic believers who support the latter? It is precisely the intent of this chapter to illustrate – albeit provisionally – the sharp fracture in the Catholic Church with regard to the interpretation and reception of the crusades.[4]

The term 'crusade' itself is divisive, since it is tied to contrasting perceptions of the medieval age of which the crusades are generally perceived as a typical expression. Such conflicting understanding has to be viewed in connection with the major event that characterised the history of the Catholic Church in the twentieth century, namely, the reforming endeavour undertaken since the Second Vatican Council (1962–65) that paved the way for a wholesale re-evaluation of the Christian past. The post-conciliar Church rejected the previous assessment of the Middle Ages, a period that was now regarded as one of the most significant phases of the 'Constantinian era' marked by a harmful entwining of spiritual and temporal matters.[5] This interpretation contrasted with the positive assessment of the medieval era faithfully nourished by the ecclesiastical hierarchy since the French Revolution. According to the 'intransigent' stance – prevailing up to the pontificate of Pius XII (r.1939–58) – the Middle Ages represent the highest expression of the 'Christendom myth'.[6] In contrast with the claims of the French Revolution, Christ's universal rulership not only extended over the spiritual field, but had to be implemented in the temporal one in order to accomplish the missionary task assigned to the Church and to prevent the frightening consequences that an estrangement from godly law would trigger.

The reception of the crusades in the contemporary Catholic Church has thus to be considered in the framework of the clash between two conflicting mind-sets. On the one hand, the intransigent standpoint, at least in official ecclesiastical statements dominant up to the Second Vatican Council, and later cultivated amongst 'traditionalist' sectors of the Church (not confined to the Lefebvrian groups). On the other, the post-conciliar perspective that dismissed several aspects of the previous position; a fact that has led many traditionalists to identify it with modernism, the set of philosophical and theological doctrines formally condemned by Pius X in 1907.[7] This position is still prevalent within the ecclesiastical hierarchy, though it is meeting with increasing resistance from the most traditionalist wings within the Church.[8] The crusades provide the perfect example of this clash, as the following pages will attempt to show.

The 'intransigent', or 'traditionalist', position

Even before the Great Jubilee of 2000, John Paul II had considered the holy wars of the past as anti-evangelical actions that required a special 'purification of memory'. The reassessment of the crusades in his teaching marked a considerable estrangement from the stance assumed by the papacy up to the Second Vatican Council. The difference can be fully grasped by looking at some episodes that occurred shortly before the Second Vatican Council itself. Less than 60 years before the solemn condemnation of the holy wars, Pius XII eulogised the deeds of the medieval crusaders, by connecting them to the missionary effort that was still ongoing in his own day: significantly, in a speech delivered in 1944, the pope maintained that the crusades were 'a most elevated and noble goal! Besides, from a historical point of view, their purpose was to defend the faith and the civilization of the Christian West against Islam'.[9] In subsequent years, Pius XII vividly fuelled the crusading ideal in more than one circumstance, giving rise to the insinuation that the announcement of a new crusade was still a possible option. In 1947, the Pontiff drew a parallel between the resistance against the Turkish onslaught at Lepanto in 1571 and the defence of Christian civilisation against the 'new infidels' – that is, the Communists: whilst addressing a group of U.S. Senators, the Pope recalled that 'the powers representing Christian civilisation united to defeat the colossal threat from the East in the battle of Lepanto'.[10] Pius XII affirmed that 7 October, the day when the battle was fought, was:

> a day of thanksgiving commemorated in the calendar of the Church, not only because the sanctuaries and altars of Europe were saved from utter destruction, but also because the prayers ordered by the then Pope St. Pius V were universally given a large share in the victory.[11]

The Pope went on to establish a clear connection to the situation in his own day: 'The day reminds Us of the most effective assistance We, successor of that other Pius, can offer to the defenders of the rights of God and man'.[12]

In the famous Christmas radio message of 1956, he evoked once again the memory of the crusades in the aftermath of the Soviet invasion of Hungary. Although he declared in the same speech that he had abstained from calling Christendom to a military effort, the crusade was in any case a possible outcome of the war that the Church had been waging against the most frightening threat posited to Christianity, namely, Communism.[13] Only two months before the above-mentioned radio message, Pius XII had beatified Innocent XI, the pope who organised the league that successfully countered the last Turkish assault in Vienna in 1683. The exaltation of this 'crusading' pope would serve the purpose to 'indicate the paths of salvation, peace and renovation to the current age, marked, like that in which he lived, by an urgent need of spiritual rebirth, by grave and heated contrasts, by huge and common dangers'.[14] A parallel between the Turks of the seventeenth century and the 'modern infidels' of Pius XII's own time, who were threatening Christianity again, was thus clearly drawn.[15]

The stance maintained by Pius XII, however, was far from innovative: in fact, it recalled a position sustained since the nineteenth century, when the struggle of the Church against secularisation was often presented in terms similar to those usually applied to the crusades. The battle against liberalism and modern liberties, which separated human society from the superior authority of the Church, understood as the sole repository of divine grace, was often perceived as a 'holy war' aimed at the restoration of the pristine medieval Christendom. This mythicised era, often described in nostalgic terms,[16] was seen as the blessed period in which the political and social spheres were together governed by the authority of the pope. According to the ecclesiological assumptions of the Catholic Church (at least before the Second Vatican Council), the vicarial participation of the Roman Pontiff in Christ's rulership made the papacy the only institution that could effectively settle conflicts between nations and states by implementing the universal kingship of Christ on earth.[17] Modern deviance was strictly tied to the estrangement from the medieval hierocratic order, from which the contemporary world had departed through a genealogy of errors that started with the Reformation, developed into the atheist philosophy that triggered the French Revolution, and culminated in the spreading of the anti-Christian ideologies of liberalism and, above all, socialism.

During the twentieth century, this struggle against the modern world in Europe was often associated by ecclesiastical authors with various expressions of fascist ideology.[18] The civil wars that ushered in the establishment of the dictatorships of Primo de Rivera and Francisco Franco in Spain were officially designated as 'crusades' by notable members of the Spanish clergy.[19] Even the Italian colonial war in Ethiopia, at a time in which the Fascist ideology had already deeply intermingled with the ecclesiastical positions in Italy,[20] was often presented as a crusading effort, aimed not only at restoring imperial Roman dignity (a concept that was enthusiastically embraced by the vast majority of Italian bishops) but also at disseminating Christian civilisation.[21] Wars, however, had already been perceived as 'crusades' in previous decades of the twentieth century, regardless of the political orientation predominant in each State: particularly during the First

World War, the conflict between the nations led on several occasions to overt clashes between their respective episcopates, a matter that elicited serious concerns on the part of the papacy.[22]

But the word 'crusade' was often used in many other occurrences in a figurative sense, to designate the spiritual fight that Catholic believers had to engage in against specific targets: a case in point was the 'crusade of prayers' to the Virgin, asked by Pius XII in order to establish world peace and to settle the contemporary plight of Palestine.[23] In this framework, it is interesting to notice a connection between a request for assistance to the Virgin and a 'crusading' effort: such relation had already been established one year before, when Pius XII specially recalled the decisive role attributed to the Mother of God in the victorious outcome of the battle of Lepanto, elicited thanks to prayers that Pius V asked to address her through the devotion of the Holy Rosary. Besides, it is not by chance that Pius XII's 'crusade of prayers', combined it with the consecration of the whole human race to the Immaculate Heart of Mary. This act could not but recall the numerous crusading expressions that had been tied to the dissemination of the cult of the Sacred Heart of Jesus between the nineteenth and the twentieth centuries;[24] not by chance, such devotion had been developing in those years in close relation with the efforts to establish the 'social kingship of Christ' against the process of secularisation.[25]

In this context, it is significant to observe the adoption of this intransigent understanding of the term 'crusade' amongst contemporary Catholic traditionalists. In particular the bishop Marcel Lefebvre, probably most representative of this current, often made use of this word to outline the struggle pursued by his fraternity against the same targets – liberalism and socialism, in their most modern expressions – that the pre-conciliar Church had indicated as its most threatening enemies. There was, however, a major difference: this crusade had to be levelled also against the modernist clergy that had taken over the Roman Curia after the Second Vatican Council, an event that, according to many traditionalist groups, marked a public treason to Catholic Tradition, especially because of the acknowledgement of human freedom (publicly admitted in the *Humanae Dignitatis*) and the introduction of ecumenism. Lefebvre's attitude was clearly expressed in a homily pronounced at Ecône shortly before his death and was synthetically reiterated in a booklet (significantly entitled *Notre Croisade*) published after his demise, where his main statements against modern civilisation and the modernist turn that had supposedly marked the post-conciliar Church were collected.[26]

In general, followers and supporters of the traditionalist wing have been the most eager to recall the memory of the crusades both in their historical relevance and in the figural signification that had already become popular during the nineteenth century. The priests of the fraternity founded by Lefebvre, in particular, were very zealous to reinstate the 'Eucharistic Crusade' launched by Pope Pius X – a figure particularly venerated by traditionalists because of his condemnation of modernism.[27] This devotion, specifically addressed to children, included a set of rules that young believers had to follow, subdivided into three degrees of perfection. Children received titles that were clearly reminiscent of medieval chivalry (page, squire, and knight), and it was precisely because of this association to the crusading language that all militant references were abandoned after the Second Vatican Council.

In this context, we should also mention the militant references associated to the devotion of the Rosary between the nineteenth and the twentieth centuries, when new private revelations attributed to the Virgin were often received as catalysts for the struggle against modern deviations, accompanied by the promise that in the end 'my Immaculate Heart will triumph', as the seers of Fátima, Portugal, reported to have heard in one of the most popular Marian apparitions of modern times.[28]

It is again amongst traditionalists that we find powerful 'crusading' references to the eschatological implications of these private revelations. Plinio Corrêa de Oliveira in particular – the founder of the conservative movement 'Tradition, Family, and Property'[29] and an author who exerted a considerable influence on several traditionalist groups, especially in Italy[30] – dedicated his major publishing efforts to outlining the successive steps that mark the historical revolutionary estrangement from the medieval *Christianitas*.[31] In doing so, he complied with the intransigent scheme that had often been updated during the twentieth century and that is still firmly held in traditionalist circles. The restoration of the Christian society has been directly associated by Corrêa de Oliveira to the revelations of the Virgin, whose 'personal triumph' announced in Fátima shall be 'the most marvellous in History'.[32]

Significantly, one of the most faithful followers of Corrêa de Oliveira, the Italian Roberto De Mattei – formerly a university professor and vice-president of the Italian *Consiglio Nazionale delle Ricerche* (National Research Council, hereafter CNR) as well as an active member of numerous traditionalist associations in Italy[33] – called him 'the Crusader of the twentieth century', thus maintaining once again that the struggle against modernity had to be understood as a 'holy war' for the defence of Christianity and the Christian vision of the human being. It is also significant that the biography of Corrêa de Oliveira written by De Mattei[34] was prefaced by Cardinal Alfons Maria Stickler, a prominent member of the Roman Curia, who had published several important scholarly essays on the juridical thought concerning the relationship between the Papacy and the Empire in the Middle Ages – thus drawing a line of conjunction between the defence of Christian tradition and the scholarly endeavour.[35]

Finally, it is not coincidental to find De Mattei personally involved in what may be called a 'rehabilitation of the crusades', especially after the Great Jubilee in 2000. On one public occasion, the Italian professor, supported by Luigi Negri, an influential Italian bishop, stated that 'the spirit of the crusades' is 'the spirit of Christianity, that is, the love for the incomprehensible mystery of the Cross'; for the crusades 'have to be understood as a category of the spirit not restricted to the Middle Ages, but the proper disposition of mind of the Christian believer'.[36] Similar re-evaluations of the crusades have been sustained by another Italian traditionalist author, Massimo Viglione – like De Mattei, also active in scholarly publications and researcher at the CNR – who in one article published online and re-posted by several other traditionalist websites, argued for the 'historical, religious and moral justification of the Crusades', maintaining that they were 'first of all wars of self-defence' (*guerre di legittima difesa*), 'aimed at reconquering what had been previously taken illegitimately by an invading enemy'.[37]

The post-conciliar perspective

It is impossible not to acknowledge the strong implicit opposition exhibited by these statements against the official teaching of John Paul II, who more than once, even before the 2000 Jubilee, firmly rejected the idea of 'holy war' and, at least on one occasion, explicitly maintained that the medieval crusade for the defence of the holy places was dissonant to the Gospel.[38] This assumption was often reiterated in subsequent declarations, especially in the framework of interreligious initiatives. In one meeting, the pope affirmed that 'every use of religion to foster violence is an abuse [...] to declare war in the name of religion is a patent contradiction'.[39] Consistently with these assumptions, John Paul II dedicated much effort to demonstrate on the world stage that different religions (and confessions within the Christian religion) could actually co-operate to promote and establish peaceful relations in the world. Such was the spirit that animated the famous prayer meetings of Assisi, organised in 1986, 1993 and 2002 (and replicated by Benedict

XVI in 2011), events to which the pope often referred as an 'essential reference for the edification of a peaceful world on the basis of the testimony of dialogue and brotherhood provided by religions'.[40]

This teaching was in line with previous theological leanings set out by the Second Vatican Council, when 'faults, flaws, "infidelity to the Spirit of God" in aspects of the Church's historical development' were admitted in the decree *Unitatis redintegratio* on ecumenism.[41] Moreover, Paul VI connected this acknowledgement of possible Catholic responsibilities in the fragmentation of Christian communities to explicit requests for forgiveness, again in relation to ecumenical efforts, aimed, in this case, at restoring unity with the Eastern Churches. In point of fact, on one occasion, he maintained that 'if we are in any way to blame for that separation, we humbly beg God's forgiveness and ask pardon too of our brethren who feel they have been injured by us'.[42]

It was, however, John Paul II who publicly introduced the expression 'purification of memory' and extended the need of a formal 'plea for forgiveness' to many other aspects of the Christian past, to the point that he formally oriented the preparation for the Great Jubilee to instilling this penitential attitude. In more than one circumstance, the pope affirmed that the Church had to 'review autonomously the *darkest aspects* of its history, evaluating them in light of the Gospel's principles'.[43] This process, which culminated in the spectacular 'Day of Pardon' on 12 March 2000, presupposed a dramatic re-evaluation of the Christian past, in terms that formally contradicted several assumptions on the Christian history formulated by previous papal teachings.[44] It seemed to confirm a 'progressive' current amongst ecclesiastical authors that emerged shortly after the end of the Second Vatican Council, strongly advocating a formal rejection of the principles on which the so-called 'Constantinian age' was grounded in order to return to the purity of the evangelical message.[45]

John Paul II's assumption was further elaborated in 2000, when the International Theological Commission, summoned by its former president, cardinal Joseph Ratzinger, included the 'use of violence at the service of truth' amongst those acts committed by Christians in the past that needed a 'purification of memory', that is, an interior disposition that:

> aims at liberating personal and communal conscience from all forms of resentment and violence that are the legacy of past faults, through a renewed historical and theological evaluation of such events. This should lead – if done correctly – to a corresponding recognition of guilt and contribute to the path of reconciliation.[46]

The document quoted extensively from John Paul's *Tertio Millennio Adveniente*, in which the pope affirmed that:

> it is appropriate that, as the Second Millennium of Christianity draws to a close, the Church should become more fully conscious of the sinfulness of her children, recalling all those times in history when they departed from the spirit of Christ and his Gospel and, instead of offering to the world the witness of a life inspired by the values of faith, indulged in ways of thinking and acting which were truly forms of counter-witness and scandal.[47]

The Commission did not provide explicit examples of these anti-evangelical deeds, but the reference to the crusades appears rather evident. As an observer very well acquainted with the Roman Curia maintains, the holy wars of the medieval and early modern ages had been 'omitted at the last minute [from the "Day of Pardon"] so as not to irritate further more than one exponent of the Curia opposed in particular to the inclusion of the crusades in the request for forgiveness'.[48] Notwithstanding the generally positive reception of John Paul II's initiative, the Commission admitted that:

> some reservations have also been voiced, mainly expressions of unease connected with particular historical and cultural contexts in which the simple admission of faults committed by the sons and daughters of the Church may look like acquiescence in the face of accusations made by those who are prejudicially hostile to the Church.[49]

Conclusion

As this chapter has illustrated, such 'reservations' – that in many cases proved to be the expression of harsh critics – has been strongly maintained by traditionalist circles, especially by those who rejected the reassessment of Christian history introduced by the Second Vatican Council and pursued during the pontificate of John Paul II. Such opposition to post-conciliar papal teaching, usually conveyed by lower strata of the ecclesiastical hierarchy and through informal and/or unofficial channels, is not limited to fringe minorities within the Catholic Church, and though traditionalist groups are numerically quite thin, their influence on various Catholic environments seems to be increasing, especially in the cultural debate, as well as in marginal but not irrelevant sections of the political life of certain Western countries, such as Italy, France and even the U.S.A. The controversy over the crusades is a case study that allows us to appreciate the scope of the struggle between post-conciliar hermeneutics and the pre-conciliar standpoint in a way that is difficult to find in other religious and cultural disputes with similarly vivid overtones.

Notes

1 Excerpt drawn from the speech of Pius XII to the Pontifical Mission Societies on Saturday, 24 June 1944, in *Discorsi e Radiomessaggi di Sua Santità Pio XII*, 6 (Rome, 1945), pp. 47–52.

2 'Day of Pardon', *The Holy See*, 12 March 2000, <https://web.archive.org/web/20190204114712/https://w2.vatican.va/content/john-paul-ii/en/homilies/2000/documents/hf_jp-ii_hom_20000312_pardon.html>, [accessed 4 February 2019].

3 'Il grande giubileo dell'anno 2000', *Il Regno/documenti* 39:15 (1994), pp. 449–54, quoted in Daniele Menozzi, *Giovanni Paolo II: Una transizione incompiuta?* (Brescia, 2006), p. 130.

4 The term 'crusade' has re-appeared periodically in ecclesiastical discourse, printed pamphlets and essays, published by Catholic authors in varied contexts. For the sake of space, we will consider mainly sources of Italian origin, due to the historically strong influence exerted by the Papacy on this country.

5 According to Marie-Dominique Chenu, who coined this expression, the 'Constantinian era' was dismantled by the Second Vatican Council: see Chenu's 'La fin de l'ère constantinienne', in *Un concile pour notre temps*, eds. Jean-Pierre Dubois-Dumée et al., vol. 2 (Paris, 1961), pp. 59–87.

6 See Giovanni Miccoli, 'Chiesa e società in Italia fra Ottocento e Novecento: Il mito della Cristianità', in Miccoli, *Fra mito della cristianità e secolarizzazione: Studi sul rapporto Chiesa-società nell'età contemporanea* (Casale Monferrato, 1985), pp. 21–92. On the development of Catholic intransigentism, see Daniele Menozzi, *La Chiesa cattolica e la secolarizzazione* (Torino, 1993), pp. 15–71.

7 On this current and its condemnation by Pius X in 1914, see, amongst others, Darrell Jodock ed., *Catholicism Contending with Modernity: Roman Catholic Modernism and Anti-Modernism in Historical Context* (Cambridge: 2000).

8 'Traditionalism' here is loosely understood as a current opposed to the spirit of the Second Vatican Council and subsequent reforms. It is usually associated with the movement founded by Marcel Lefebvre, but in reality, it includes several other milieus that belong to 'conservative Catholicism'. See Menozzi, *La Chiesa cattolica e la secolarizzazione*, pp. 198–231; Nicla Buonasorte, *Tra Roma e Lefebvre: Il tradizionalismo cattolico e il Concilio Vaticano II* (Rome, 2003); Giovanni Miccoli, *La Chiesa dell'anticoncilio: I tradizionalisti alla riconquista di Roma* (Roma-Bari, 2011).

9 *Discorsi*, 6 (1945), pp. 47–52.

10 'Parole di Sua Santità Pio XII ad un gruppo di senatori e di rappresentanti del Congresso degli Stati Uniti appartenenti al "Committee Investigating Information Program"', in *Discorsi e Radiomessaggi di Sua Santità Pio XII*, 9 (Rome, 1948), p. 271.

11 Ibid.

12 Ibid.

13 'Radiomessaggio di Sua Santità Pio PP. XII ai fedeli e al popolo del mondo intero', in *Discorsi e radiomessaggi di Sua Santità Pio XII* 18 (Rome, 1957), p. 736.

14 'Radiomessaggio di Sua Santità Pio PP. XII in onore del beato Innocenzo XI', in *Discorsi*, 18 (1957), p. 532.

15 See Rachael Pymm's chapter in this volume, p. 91.

16 See Raoul Manselli, 'Il Medioevo come "Christianitas": Una scoperta romantica', in *Concetto, storia, miti e immagini del Medio Evo: Atti del XIV Corso Internazionale d'Alta Cultura*, ed. Vittore Branca (Florence, 1973), pp. 51–89.

17 Pius XII himself expressed this idea in his speech to the Swiss pilgrims convened in Rome to celebrate the canonisation of Nicholas of Flüe: see 'Discorso di Sua Santità Pio XII ai pellegrini elvetici', in *Discorsi e radiomessaggi di Pio XII* 9 (Rome, 1948), pp. 71–80.

18 See Daniele Menozzi and Renato Moro, eds., *Cattolicesimo e totalitarismo: Chiese e culture religiose tra le due guerre mondiali (Italia, Spagna, Francia)* (Brescia, 2004).

19 There are several important publications on this topic, especially in Spanish and Italian. See, for instance, Hilari Raguer, *La pólvora y el incienso: La Iglesia y la guerra civil española (1936–1939)* (Barcelona, 2001); Alfonso Botti, 'Dalla "guerra giusta" alla "guerra santa": La pubblicistica cattolica spagnola durante la Seconda repubblica e la guerra civile', *Storia e problemi contemporanei* 42 (2006), pp. 61–91.

20 See, amongst others, Renato Moro, 'L'opinione cattolica su pace e guerra durante il fascismo', in *Chiesa e guerra*, pp. 221–319.

21 Italian missionaries in Ethiopia did not hesitate to coin a clearly crusades-related expression ('Gesta Dei per Italos!') to celebrate the providential inspiration of the Italian colonial endeavour: see Lucia Ceci, 'La Chiesa e la questione colonial: Guerra e missione nell'impresa d'Etiopia', in *Chiesa e guerra*, p. 345.

22 See, for instance, Vincent Viaene, 'Catholic Attitude towards War and Peace from the "fin-de-siècle" to World War I: The French Case', *Revue d'histoire ecclésiastique* 89 (1994), pp. 390–411; Roberto Morozzo della Rocca, 'Benedetto XV e la sacralizzazione della prima guerra mondiale', in *Chiesa e guerra*, pp. 165–81.

23 In the encyclical *Auspicia quaedam*, 1 May 1948. See *Acta Apostolicae Sedis* 40 (1948), pp. 169–72.

24 The relation between the consecration of human kind to the Sacred Heart of Jesus and to the Immaculate Heart of Mary was clearly outlined by Pius XII: 'And even as our predecessor of immortal memory, Leo XIII, at the dawn of the twentieth century saw fit to consecrate the whole human race to the Most Sacred Heart of Jesus, so We have likewise, in the guise of representative of the whole human family which He redeemed, desired to dedicate it in turn to the Immaculate Heart of the Virgin Mary' (Pius XII, 'Auspicia quaedam', p. 172).

25 For this cult and its manifold theological-political implications, see the fundamental work of Daniele Menozzi, *Sacro Cuore: Un culto tra devozione interiore e restaurazione cristiana della società* (Rome, 2001).

26 Marcel Lefebvre, *Notre Croisade* (Nouan-le-Fuzelier, 1997).

27 On the origins of this devotion, see Ludovic Laloux, 'Aux origines de la Croisade eucharistique: Un soutien aux poilus lors de la Grande Guerre', *Guerres mondiales et conflits contemporains*, 219 (2005), pp. 45–51. On the support of the Eucharistic Crusade by Fraternity Pius X founded by Mgr. Lefebvre, see 'Statuts de la Croisade Eucharistique', <https://web.archive.org/web/20190201160857/http://www.seminaire-econe.ch/frcom/statuts_fr.htm>, [accessed 1 February 2019]; for the reception of this devotion by another anti-conciliar group, see 'Croisade eucharistique', *Sodalitium*, <https://web.archive.org/web/20190201160903/http://www.sodalitium.eu/croisade-eucharistique/>, [accessed 1 February 2019].

28 On the apparitions of Fátima, see Jeffrey S. Bennett, *When the Sun Danced: Myth, Miracles, and Modernity in Early Twentieth-Century Portugal* (Charlottesville, 2012).

29 Aside from apologetic publications, scholarly publications dedicated to Corrêa de Oliveira and his organisation are scanty. See Filipe Francisco Neves Domingues da Silva, 'Cruzados do século XX: O movimento tradição, família e propriedade (TFP). Origens, doutrinas e práticas (1960–1970)', MA Dissertation (Universidade Federal de Pernambuco, 2009).

30 The most significant Italian group influenced by Corrêa de Oliveira is the organisation 'Alleanza Cattolica', which collects of vast group of believers and has included several academic scholars of national and international reputation, such as Massimo Introvigne, founder of CESNUR (Centro studi sulle nuove religioni) and vice president of 'Alleanza' until 2016; Marco Tangheroni, professor of Medieval History at the University of Pisa until his death in 2004; and PierLuigi Zoccatelli, currently professor of Sociology of Religion at the Salesian Pontifical University in Rome. Several publications of Corrêa were hosted in *Cristianità*, the official journal of *Alleanza Cattolica*. See <http://alleanzacattolica.org/plinio-correa-de-oliveira/> and <http://alleanzacattolica.org/plinio-correa-de-oliveira-1908-1995/> [accessed 17 September 2018], both articles written by Giovanni Cantoni, founder and president of 'Alleanza' until 2016.

31 This is especially the topic of his work *Revolução e Contra-Revolução* (São Paulo, 1998), originally published for the monthly 'Catolicismo' in 1959 and subsequently re-edited until the final version of 1998.

32 Roberto De Mattei, *Plinio Corrêa de Oliveira: Apostolo di Fatima, Profeta del Regno di Maria* (Rome, 2017), p. 327.

33 Such as 'Corrispondenza Romana', named after the review of the integrist Umberto Benigni, and the 'Lepanto Foundation', whose magazine *Lepanto* dedicated the first issue to Corrêa de Oliveira.

34 Roberto De Mattei, *Il crociato del secolo XX: Plinio Corrêa de Oliveira* (Casale Monferrato, 1996).

35 Amongst his most important works, see Sacerdotium et Regnum *nei decretisti e primi decretalisti: Considerazioni metodologiche di ricerca e testi* (Torino, 1953).

36 Silvia Franzoni, 'Il vescovo Negri e il prof. de Mattei parlano sulle crociate', *Corrispondenza Romana*, 12 November 2014, <https://web.archive.org/web/20190201161934/https://www.corrispondenzaromana.it/il-vescovo-negri-e-il-prof-de-mattei-parlano-sulle-crociate/>, [accessed 1 February 2019]. Very similar sentences are reported in Roberto De Mattei, *Guerra santa, guerra giusta: Islam e cristianesimo in guerra* (Casale Monferrato, 2002),

p. 7. For a critical comment on this book from a scholarly perspective, see Alfonso Marini, 'Storia contestata: Francesco d'Assisi e l'Islam', *Franciscana* 14 (2012), p. 15, n. 40.

37 Massimo Viglione, 'La legittimità storica, religiosa e morale delle crociate', *Il Giudizio Cattolico*, <https://web.archive.org/web/20180615191305/http://www.ilgiudiziocattolico.com/1/34/la-legittimit%C3%A0-storica-religiosa-e-morale-delle-crociate.html>, [accessed 1 February 2019]. Small traditionalist groups in America are also trying to restore an organised Catholic militia: see the presentation of the recently established 'Ordo Militaris Catholicus', aimed at organising 'an actual fighting force of armed Catholic men dedicated to defending the persecuted faithful', in 'total conformity to U.S. Laws' and 'based upon [the] Rule of the Knights Templar' (see André Marie, 'A New Order of Crusaders, Seriously!', Catholicism.org, 20 September 2016, <https://web.archive.org/web/20190201163556/https://catholicism.org/ad-rem-no-277.html>, and Ordo Militaris, <https://web.archive.org/web/20190201163402/https://www.ordo-militaris.us/>, [both accessed 1 February 2019].

38 See Erminio Lora, ed., *Enchiridion della pace, vol. 2: Paolo VI-Giovanni Paolo II* (Bologna, 2004), p. 3809; Daniele Menozzi, *Giovanni Paolo II: Una transizione incompiuta?* (Brescia, 2006), p. 89.

39 *Enchiridion della pace*, p. 4445, quoted in Menozzi, *Giovanni Paolo II*, p. 89.

40 Ibid., p. 91.

41 Ibid., p. 127, who refers in this quotation to a passage of the Constitution *Gaudium et Spes* (Ch. 43).

42 *Insegnamenti di Paolo VI*, 8 (Vatican City, 1970), p. 674, quoted in Menozzi, *Giovanni Paolo II*, p. 128. Similar statements were later made when Paul VI announced that the excommunication that separated the Catholic and the Orthodox churches had been revoked: see *Insegnamenti di Paolo VI*, 3 (Vatican City, 1965), p. 736.

43 'Il grande giubileo dell'anno 2000', *Il Regno/documenti* 39:15 (1994), pp. 449–54, quoted in Menozzi, *Giovanni Paolo II*, p. 133. Emphasis original.

44 Ibid., pp. 136–7.

45 Ibid., p. 130.

46 Commissione Teologica Internazionale, 'Memoria e riconciliazione: La Chiesa e le colpe del passato', *La Civiltà Cattolica* 151:5 (2000), p. 468.

47 Pope John Paul II, *Tertio Millennio Adveniente*, 10 November 1994, 33, *Acta Apostolicae Sedis* 87 (1995), p. 25. Emphasis original.

48 Gianfranco Brunelli, 'The Great Jubilee of Pope Wojtyla', *Italian Politics* 16 (2001), p. 158. Several English-speaking authors have contended that an explicit condemnation of the crusades was not, in fact, issued by John Paul II. Andrew Holt, for instance, maintains that the plea for forgiveness (understood within a 'liberating process of purification of memory') addressed by the Pope to the Patriarch of Constantinople for the crimes and abuses committed during the Fourth Crusade 'was not an apology for the crusades [...] or the principle of crusading itself' (see Andrew Holt, 'Apology for the Fourth Crusade', *apholt.com*, <https://web.archive.org/web/20190201164158/https://apholt.com/2016/05/26/apology-for-the-fourth-crusade/>, [accessed 1 February 2019]. See also Thomas F. Madden, 'Crusade Myths', *Ignatius Insight* <https://web.archive.org/web/20190201164429/http://www.ignatiusinsight.com/features2005/

88   *Marco Giardini*

tmadden_crusademyths_feb05.asp>, [accessed 1 February 2019]. These statements, however, do not seem to take into account the broader set of declarations issued by John Paul II on religious wars of the past, only a short part of which have been reported in this chapter.
49 'Memoria e riconciliazione', p. 469.

Bibliography

Primary

Cantoni, Giovanni. 'Plinio Corrêa de Oliveira (1908–1995)', *Alleanza Cattolica*, http://alleanzacattolica.org/plinio-correa-de-oliveira-1908-1995/. [Accessed 17 September 2018].
———. 'Plinio Corrêa de Oliveira'. *Alleanza Cattolica*. http://alleanzacattolica.org/plinio-correa-de-oliveira/. [Accessed 17 September 2018].
Chenu, Marie-Dominique. 'La fin de l'ère constantinienne'. In *Un concile pour notre temps*, eds. Jean-Pierre Dubois-Dumée et alii. Paris: Éditions du Cerf, 1961. pp. 59–87.
Commissione Teologica Internazionale. 'Memoria e riconciliazione: La Chiesa e le colpe del passato', *La Civiltà Cattolica* 151:5 (2000), pp. 468–508.
Corrêa de Oliveira, Plinio. *Revolução e Contra-Revolução*. São Paulo: Artpress, 1998.
De Mattei, Roberto. *Il crociato del secolo XX: Plinio Corrêa de Oliveira*. Casale Monferrato: Piemme, 1996.
———. *Guerra santa, guerra giusta: Islam e cristianesimo in guerra*. Casale Monferrato: Piemme, 2002.
———. *Plinio Corrêa de Oliveira: Apostolo di Fatima, Profeta del Regno di Maria*. Rome: Edizioni Fiducia, 2017.
Franzoni, Silvia. 'Il vescovo Negri e il prof. de Mattei parlano sulle crociate'. *Corrispondenza Romana*. 12 November 2014. https://web.archive.org/web/20190201161934/https://www.corrispondenzaromana.it/il-vescovo-negri-e-il-prof-de-mattei-parlano-sulle-crociate/. [Accessed 1 February 2019].
Holt, Andrew. 'Apology for the Fourth Crusade'. *apholt.com*. https://web.archive.org/web/20190201164158/https://apholt.com/2016/05/26/apology-for-the-fourth-crusade/. [Accessed 1 February 2019].
Istituto Mater Boni Consilii. 'Croisade eucharistique'. *Sodalitium*. https://web.archive.org/web/20190201160903/http://www.sodalitium.eu/croisade-eucharistique/. [Accessed 1 February 2019].
John Paul II. 'Il grande giubileo dell'anno 2000', *Il Regno/documenti* 39:15 (1994), pp. 449–54.
———. *Tertio Millennio Adveniente*, 10 November 1994, 33, *Acta Apostolicae Sedis* 87 (1995), p. 25.
———. 'Day of Pardon'. *The Holy See*. 12 March 2000. https://web.archive.org/web/20190204114712/https://w2.vatican.va/content/john-paul-ii/en/homilies/2000/documents/hf_jp-ii_hom_20000312_pardon.html. [Accessed 4 February 2019].

Lefebvre, Marcel. *Notre croisade.* Nouan-le-Fuzelier: Éditions du Lion de Juda, 1997.

Lora, Erminio, ed. *Enchiridion della pace, Volume 2: Paolo VI-Giovanni Paolo II.* Bologna: EDB, 2004.

Madden, Thomas F. Madden. 'Crusade Myths'. *Ignatius Insight.* https:// web.archive.org/web/20190201164429/http://www.ignatiusinsight.com/ features2005/tmadden_crusademyths_feb05.asp. [Accessed 1 February 2019].

Marie, André. 'A New Order of Crusaders, Seriously!'. *Catholicism.org.* 20 September 2016. https://web.archive.org/web/20190201163556/https:// catholicism.org/ad-rem-no-277.html. [Accessed 1 February 2019].

Ordo Militaris. https://web.archive.org/web/20190201163402/https://www.ordo- militaris.us/. [Accessed 1 February 2019].

Paul VI. *Insegnamenti di Paolo VI.* Vols 3 and 8. Vatican City, Libreria Editrice Vaticana, 1965, 1970.

Pius XII. *Discorsi e radiomessaggi di Sua Santità Pio XII.* Vols 6, 9, and 18. Rome, Tipografia Poliglotta Vaticana, 1945, 1948, 1957.

Pius XII. 'Encyclical "Auspicia quaedam"'. *Acta Apostolicae Sedis* 40 (1948), pp. 169–72.

'Statuts de la Croisade Eucharistique'. *Séminaire d'Écône.* https://web.archive. org/web/20190201160857/http://www.seminaire-econe.ch/frcom/statuts_ fr.htm. [Accessed 1 February 2019].

Viglione, Massimo. 'La legittimità storica, religiosa e morale delle crociate'. *Il Giudizio Cattolico.* https://web.archive.org/web/20180615191305/http:// www.ilgiudiziocattolico.com/1/34/la-legittimit%C3%A0-storica-religiosa- e-morale-delle-crociate.html. [Accessed 1 February 2019].

Secondary

Botti, Alfonso. 'Dalla "guerra giusta" alla "guerra santa": La pubblicistica cattolica spagnola durante la Seconda repubblica e la guerra civile'. *Storia e problemi contemporanei* 42 (2006), pp. 61–91.

Brunelli, Gianfranco. 'The Great Jubilee of Pope Wojtyla'. *Italian Politics* 16 (2001), pp. 151–67.

Buonasorte, Nicla. *Tra Roma e Lefebvre: Il tradizionalismo cattolico e il Con- cilio Vaticano II.* Rome: Studium, 2003.

Casali, Luciano. 'L'ultima crociata'. In *Dai cantieri della storia: Liber amico- rum per Paolo Prodi,* eds. Gian Paolo Brizzi and Giuseppe Olmi. Bologna: CLUEB, 2007. pp. 191–202.

De Giorgi, Fulvio. 'Linguaggi militari e mobilitazione cattolica nell'Italia fascista'. *Contemporanea* 5:2 (2002), pp. 253–86.

Domingues da Silva, Filipe Francisco Neves. 'Cruzados do século XX: O movimento tradição, família e propriedade (TFP). Origens, doutrinas e práticas (1960–1970)'. MA Dissertation (Universidade Federal de Pernam- buco, 2009).

Jodock, Darrell, ed. *Catholicism Contending with Modernity: Roman Catholic Modernism and Anti-Modernism in Historical Context.* Cambridge: CUP, 2000.

Laloux, Ludovic. 'Aux origines de la Croisade eucharistique: Un soutien aux poilus lors de la Grande Guerre'. *Guerres mondiales et conflits contemporains* 219 (2005), pp. 45–51.

Manselli, Raoul. 'Il Medioevo come "Christianitas": Una scoperta romantica'. In *Concetto, storia, miti e immagini del Medio Evo: Atti del XIV Corso Internazionale d'Alta Cultura*, ed. Vittore Branca. Florence: Sansoni, 1973. pp. 51–89.

Marini, Alfonso. 'Storia contestata: Francesco d'Assisi e l'Islam'. *Franciscana* 14 (2012), pp. 1–54.

Menozzi, Daniele. *La Chiesa cattolica e la secolarizzazione*. Torino: Einaudi, 1993.

———. *Giovanni Paolo II: Una transizione incompiuta?* Brescia: Morcelliana, 2006.

Menozzi, Daniele, and Renato Moro, eds. *Cattolicesimo e totalitarismo: Chiese e culture religiose tra le due guerre mondiali (Italia, Spagna, Francia)*. Brescia: Morcelliana, 2004.

Miccoli, Giovanni. *Fra mito della cristianità e secolarizzazione: Studi sul rapporto Chiesa-società nell'età contemporanea*. Casale Monferrato: Marietti, 1985.

———. *La Chiesa dell'anticoncilio: I tradizionalisti alla riconquista di Roma*. Rome-Bari: Laterza, 2011.

Moro, Renato. 'L'opinione cattolica su pace e guerra durante il fascismo'. In *Chiesa e guerra: Dalla 'benedizione delle armi' alla 'Pacem in terris'*, eds. Mimmo Franzinelli and Riccardo Bottoni. Bologna: Il Mulino, 2005. pp. 221–319.

Raguer, Hilari. *La pólvora y el incienso: La Iglesia y la guerra civil española (1936–1939)*. Barcelona: Ediciones Península, 2001.x

Viaene, Vincent. 'Catholic Attitude towards War and Peace from the "fin-de-siècle" to World War I: The French Case'. *Revue d'histoire ecclésiastique* 89 (1994), pp. 390–411.

6   Philatelic depictions of the crusades

Rachael Pymm

National memories of the crusades have been communicated in a variety of ways in the centuries since the campaigns themselves. A previously unexamined context is the expression of national memories of the crusades via the rhetoric and artwork on, or associated with, modern postage stamps. A consideration of philatelic depictions of the crusades provides insight into both the different ways in which the crusades have been viewed and reinterpreted for modern usage, and the way in which a country has memorialised and communicated its involvement in the medieval crusades. Postage stamps are a ubiquitous element of modern life, used to prove the prepaid fee for carriage of a letter or parcel through national and international postal systems. First introduced in Great Britain on 1 May 1840, in the form of the famous Penny Black, they are now used globally. Postage stamps are usually small and rectangular with perforated edges, but other shapes including circles and hearts (and from Tonga, birds and fruit) have entered the market. According to the Convention of the Universal Postal Union (UPU) – a U.N. agency that coordinates the worldwide postal system and postal policies between the 192 member-nations – stamps must include a value indicator, the name of the issuing country (exempting Great Britain) and a design.[1] The latter element is a visual representation that reflects something of how a country wishes to portray itself – both to its own citizens and to the rest of the world at large.

The images on postage stamps are advertisements or propaganda for the country of origin, communicating messages regarding culture, tourism, economy, religion and politics.[2] However, as postage stamps have become commonplace in society, we rarely consider them as such. It has been aptly remarked:

> We see and use stamps frequently, but rarely stop to think of their rich imagery and multiple messages [...] The mundane character and our individual ways of looking hide the stamps' status as

official visual images, because they are documents produced, or at least authorized, by the state. [...] They are the way in which the state visually presents (or misrepresents) its history, culture, society, and its place in the world.[3]

When studied as tools of nation-building, a much more profound insight into stamp artwork is gained. It is possible to discern how representations of national achievements, heroes, locations, heritage and pastimes can provide a source of pride and national unity for domestic citizens, and an advertisement to the international community. Such a message can be further reinforced through the same medium by other postal elements, such as temporary cancellations which, when used most effectively, can bolster and enhance the message of a stamp. A consideration of the crusades as portrayed in philately provides an insight into three areas: the use of the term 'crusade' in the twentieth and twenty-first centuries; the use of imagined medievalised images of the crusades in communication of modern messages; and how a country chooses to commemorate and communicate its participation in the medieval crusades.

Campaigning crusader medievalism

When it appears on postage stamps, the word 'crusade' is usually used in a metaphorical or secular sense,[4] indicative of a campaign for change, devoid of the religious features of the medieval crusades. The arenas of the desired change are broad in scope, covering social, health and political spheres, which attest to the perceived reach and influence that postage stamps have, or are hoped to have. In 1945, France issued a stamp titled *Croisade de l'air pur* ('crusade for clean air'), which depicted two happy children running in the open countryside (Figure 6.1). It is a 4 plus 2-*franc* stamp, indicating that it is a semi-postal, or charity stamp, and was sold at a premium over the postal rate (4 *francs*), with the excess (2 *francs*) being donated to the charity. At this time, 4 *francs* would carry a 50-g letter nationally[5]; thus, its message was primarily directed domestically. During the Second World War, the Vichy government of France sought to promote national solidarity and mutual help through a series of propaganda campaigns.[6] In 1942, a film entitled *La Croisade de l'air pur* was released. It showed the activities of the French National Relief 'in run-down neighbourhoods, where children were suffering malnutrition and lack of fresh air',[7] and juxtaposed this with images of summer camps, to the goal of enticing the viewer to solidarity in winning this 'crusade'.[8] It is likely that, three years later,

Figure 6.1 Croisade de l'air pur, 1945, France. Artist: Achille Ouvré. © *La Poste*, 2017. From author's personal collection. Used by kind permission of *La Poste.*

a subtle visual reminder in the morning's post helped to keep the message alive. In this instance, the term 'crusade' was employed to reinforce a national campaign for social change and health.

In 1941, a set of four stamps was issued in Romania, which bore the legend *razboul sfant contra bolshevismului* ('the holy war against Bolshevism'), thus demonstrating the use of crusade rhetoric in philately to support a political aim. At this time, Romania, under the leadership of Ion Antonescu (1882–1946), was allied to the Axis powers of Germany, Italy and Japan. In the summer of 1941, 325,685 Romanians participated in Operation Barbarossa[9] – the military campaign launched by Nazi Germany against the Soviet Union. The name 'Barbarossa' deliberately recalled the twelfth-century German, Holy Roman Emperor Frederick I (1122–90), nicknamed Barbarossa, who went on crusade.[10] Additionally, Nazi propaganda actively promoted the war in the east as a 'crusade against Bolshevism'.[11] Therefore, the Romanian use of this rhetoric demonstrated the country's alliance with Nazi Germany, and the adoption and promotion of the same propaganda. In stark contrast, a few years later, the rhetoric of crusade was used in a political context for the entirely opposite aim of promoting peace: the 1947 *Cruzada escolar Argentina por la paz mundial* ('Argentine Children's Crusade for World Peace') stamps were issued to support President Juan Perón's (1895–1974), earlier speech calling for world peace.[12]

There is an element of overlap between the secular use of the word 'crusade' on stamps and imagined medievalised images of the crusades in their artwork. Most stamp designs are generated by contracted artists, and thus most graphics are artistic renditions of the subject matter. A series of stamps bearing the text *Cruzada contra el frio* ('Crusade against the cold') were produced in 1936–9 at the direction of Nationalist leader General Emilio Mola y Vidal (1887–1937) during the Spanish Civil War.[13] They are not strictly postage stamps, but revenue, fiscal or tax stamps – they did not replace the official Spanish stamps, but their use was obligatory alongside Spanish stamps on envelopes sent from Nationalist-controlled areas. The 10 *centimos* charge for each tax stamp raised funds for warm winter clothes for the Nationalist forces, and their circulation was intended to raise awareness and support for the troops. Whilst most of them feature Civil War soldiers, one issued in 1937 depicts a crusader on horseback. The image is detailed and dynamic; the horse rears upon its hind legs, conveying a sense of action and drama. The horse is wearing a caparison, common from the late twelfth century, and the rider is wearing full armour, an elaborately plumed helmet and carries a shield and polearm. This image, alongside the slogan, reinforced the association of the medieval crusades with the Civil War. The language of crusade and Spanish crusade iconography was used to great effect by the Nationalist forces throughout this campaign.[14] In the 1940s, Franco was depicted as the focus and centrepiece of a mural entitled *Franco: Victor of the Crusade,* and in 1955 he unveiled a statute of El Cid (Rodrigo Díaz de Vivar, *c.* 1043–99) and presented himself as a modern-day equivalent.[15] Being unofficial, the history of the production of the *cruzada contra el frio* stamps is revealing: the stamp depicting the crusader was designed by 'Ibánez', presumably a Nationalist supporter. Not having access to the government's printing presses, the stamps were printed lithographically by the Hija de B. Fournier company (c. 1900–78), famous for producing playing cards. The company was located in Burgos, northern Spain – the childhood home and final resting place of El Cid; it may be, therefore, that the image on the stamp is a representation of El Cid.[16]

Imagery associating the medieval crusades with a modern societal adversary is most often employed in the arena of health. A 1934 one-penny (1d) semi-postal or charity stamp, from New Zealand – a country with no direct association with the medieval crusades – depicts a crusader on horseback marching under the banner for health (Figure 6.2). The crosses on his shield and hauberk are features common to the imagined image of a crusader and help identify him specifically as such, rather than simply a mounted knight.

The same year, Belgium produced a series of stamps which bore a very similar image of a crusader (Figure 6.3). These stamps were also semi-postals with a 10 *cents* surcharge to generate funds for the

Figure 6.2 Crusade for Health, 1934, New Zealand. From author's personal collection. Used by kind permission of New Zealand Post.

Figure 6.3 Health Crusader, 1934, Belgium. © bpost, used by kind permission. Author's personal collection.

anti-tuberculosis campaign. There were seven stamps in this series, each with the same graphic, printed in a different colour according to the value. The image is of a crusader on horseback, but whereas the New Zealand stamp shows the character and horse in full, the Belgian stamp shows only the upper section. The knight carries a large shield, situated in the foreground of the stamp, which bears a double-barred cross printed in a bright red. Due to the surrounding white space of the shield interior and the contrast provided by detailed nature of the coloured design, the symbol is rendered particularly prominent and eye-catching.

The double-barred cross, also called the Lorraine cross, is associated with the crusades and was said to have been adopted as the standard of Godfrey of Bouillon (1060–1100), famed member of the First Crusade and first ruler of the Latin Kingdom of Jerusalem, as the emblem of his house.[17] On this stamp, the cross is a key feature identifying the knight as a crusader. The double-barred cross is, in fact, a symbol of anti-tuberculosis stamp issues worldwide – it was adopted as the symbol of the Central Bureau for Prevention of Tuberculosis, the forerunner to the modern International Union against Tuberculosis and Lung Disease, in 1902. Although the International Union makes no such claims, it is thought that the symbol was proposed in emulation of Godfrey of Bouillon, the double-barred cross signifying courage and success to crusaders.[18] The records of the 1902 conference, however, do not support this. The international co-operative efforts against the disease are clearly described as a crusade throughout the proceedings, and the symbol's proposer Dr. Gilbert Sesiron named them a 'peaceful crusade'. He suggested the 'Double Red Cross' as an 'emblem of peace and of fraternal understanding' and exhorted attendees to 'Use it to mark your daily conquests, and your march onward throughout the world will be a triumph over your deadly foe'. Yet, despite all the associative language and imagery, explicit connection with the medieval crusades or Godfrey of Bouillon is absent from the symbol's proposition.[19]

Significantly, in all the examples noted above, the crusader is equated with country of origin, and the affliction – be it the cold, poor health or disease – is the enemy. Additionally, each issue tacitly associates the crusades with charity and benevolent enterprises; this demonstrates a supposition that the originating nation viewed the crusades sympathetically at that time, and either considered them, interpreted them, or sought to highlight their supposed features as altruistic or charitable endeavours.

Nationalising the crusades

Overall, the proportion of worldwide stamps and other philatelic elements issued since the late nineteenth century which depict the crusades are small. Of these, a surprising number have been generated for the philatelic market – high-value stamps that were prepared just to be sold to collectors and did not see any postal use within the issuing country. They frequently bear the names of countries that have no direct association with the subject matter, including Dominica, Guyana, Lesotho, Somalia and Senegal. In 1999, the latter produced a set of three minisheets, totalling 27 different stamps, depicting characters from the crusades as chess pieces (Figure 6.4). As the primary market for these is collectors, such issues cannot inform us as to the stamp-issuing entity's engagement with the crusades, or the messages they were seeking to convey, as these factors were simply irrelevant to the issuing of the stamp.

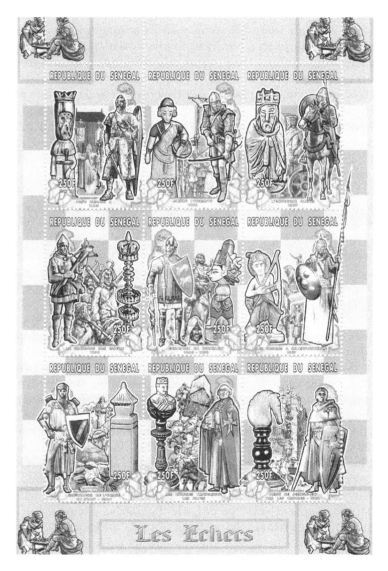

Figure 6.4 Les Echecs, 1999, Senegal. Author's personal collection.

Conversely, the Sovereign Order of Malta, which celebrates its origin in the medieval crusader states, has a strong claim to a crusading heritage, yet is a 'non-state entity subject to international law'.[20] The Order established its own postal service in the sixteenth century and has issued modern postage stamps since 1966 – although its right to do so is ornamental.[21] Imitating modern nation-states, the Order's stamps feature its 'history, its charitable and humanitarian works, its artistic heritage, Religion [sic]'.[22] References to its crusading past depicted through stamps project a historical continuity with the crusades and crusaders and reinforce the perception of a crusading identity to the Order's members and the international community alike.

To examine a national memory of the crusades as depicted in philately, a systematic analysis of a country's issues was required, and for this purpose, France was selected. The French government had maintained control of French postal service, currently named *La Poste,* until 2010, when it became a public limited company; thus, stamp issues to 2010 could be considered government approved. Stamps issued thereafter are still arguably reflections of national perspectives but are distanced from the authorisation of the state. The first French postage stamp was issued in 1849, nine years after the Penny Black of Great Britain. Following the First World War, diversity in French stamp design increased, as did the number of new releases. Numbers issued rose gradually in the decades of the twentieth century, from an average of 24 issues per year in the 1930s, reaching a peak of 362 in 2008.[23]

Stamps depicting medieval history account for a small proportion of all stamp issues, and the crusades form an even smaller subset. Being already so narrowly defined, the classifications used are two: crusade-related and crusade-specific images, with the latter having the greatest significance. Crusade-related stamps depict persons and locales that are familiar to crusade historians, but the image itself is not related to the crusades. An example would be the 1953 French stamp depicting St. Bernard of Clairvaux (1090–1153). St. Bernard famously preached the Second Crusade, but his influence extended to other spheres of church and political history. The stamp shows a portrait of the subject surrounded by a halo, and there are no elements of the design, which specifically equate St. Bernard with the crusade. Similarly, stamps featuring medieval French kings who went on crusade, or locations associated with the medieval crusades, would be classified as crusade related unless the image itself clearly references the crusades, as these persons and places have a broad history to draw from. The crusade-specific stamps of France are few compared to the total output, but nonetheless their contribution is significant. The design of French crusade-specific stamps and postal elements, and the timing of their issue, serves to illustrate French national perceptions of the crusades at points during the twentieth and early twenty-first centuries. We are thereby able to identify subtle changes to the way in which a country has interpreted and expressed national involvement in the medieval crusades, and the modern uses to which medievalised crusade imagery has been put.

Shortly after the close of the Second World War, in 1946, a 'Crusade for Peace' was organised at Vézelay, in northern France, the site at which Bernard of Clairvaux preached the Second Crusade 800 years earlier. Its genesis has been ascribed to the 1942 Christmas Day message of Pope Pius XII (1876–1958; pontifex 1939–58),[24] in which he exhorted Christians 'filled with the enthusiasm of Crusaders, to unite in the spirit of truth, justice and love to the call; God wills it, ready to serve, to sacrifice themselves, like the Crusaders of old'; the aim was to:

> traverse the sea of errors of our day and to march on to free the holy land of the spirit [...] The essential aim of this necessary and holy crusade is that the Star of Peace [...] may shine out again over the whole [of] mankind.[25]

It has been suggested that Paul Doncœur (1880–1961), Jesuit and chaplain of the *Scouts de France* (French Scouts), organised the event.[26] It is clear that he gave an address at the event,[27] which does bear similarities to other such public religious events and pilgrimages in which Doncœur was involved, each with the aim of restoring a sense of community and spiritual renewal.[28] An expectant participant described the crusade as 'a different kind of crusade [...] a crusade of prayer, and penitence, and action, for peace [...] its object is world-peace'.[29] 40,000 pilgrims are said to have attended,[30] bringing with them 14 crosses representing countries of Europe – a 15th was contributed at the last minute by German prisoners of war. Philatelically, the Crusade for Peace was marked by two circular commemorative handstamps (cancellation markings applied manually), which were applied to all mail sent from Vézelay on 21 and 22 July 1946. The first bears the text *Croisade de la Paix, Vezelay*, encircling the image of a dove holding an olive branch – both symbols of peace – atop a chalice, designed to reflect the religious nature of the occasion. The second handstamp appears to depict Bernard of Clairvaux and bears the text *8° centenaire 2ᵉ croisade, Vézelay* ('Eight-hundredth centenary of the Second Crusade, Vézelay'). It is also interesting to note that this handstamp represents the first historical event ever given a commemorative cancellation in France.

The Crusade for Peace was also celebrated by a set of commemorative labels, which look similar to postage stamps but were not valid for postage as they omit key features, such as a value indicator and the country name. The labels depict a cross moline, centred in the archway of a building. *8° centenaire 2ᵉ croisade* is written in the semicircular arch, and *Dieu le Veut* ('God wills it') between the arch and the cross. This wording is interesting as it is a battle cry more commonly associated with the First Crusade, but may perhaps also refer to the 1942 Christmas message of Pope Pius XII. At the foot of the cross are the dates 1146 and 1946 and the word 'Vézelay'. Thus, at this time, the crusades – perhaps somewhat antonymously – were invoked in the service of a zeal for and spirit of peace, and as a source of inspiration for unity and brotherhood transcending class boundaries.[31] The fortuitous timing of the eight-hundredth centenary of the launch of the Second Crusade, at the accessible physical location of Vézelay, combined with an ideology which struck a chord with European Catholics, provided the perfect conditions for this event, which was clearly of sufficient national significance to warrant commemorative handstamps.

Two years later, the Seventh Crusade was similarly commemorated by a handstamp cancellation applied to mail from Joinville, Haute Marne, over 11–12 July 1948. It bore text explicitly commemorating the crusade, accompanied by an image of Jean de Joinville (1224–1317), lord of Joinville and seneschal of Champagne. In the footsteps of his father, Joinville joined the Seventh Crusade in the service of King Louis IX. Joinville survived the expedition and, in the final years of his life, wrote of his experiences. The text *Commemoration VIIᵉ Croisade* and *Joinville (H.M.)* encircle an image of the head and torso of man, turned away such that part of his back faces the viewer, stooped slightly, he looks down at the date 11–12 July 1946. The likeness was taken from the statue of Joinville in Haute Marne.

Joinville is also the first individual who appears on a crusade-specific postage stamp (Figure 6.5). In 1957, France released a set of six stamps titled *Célébrités* (celebrities), each with a surcharge to raise money for the *Croix-Rouge français* (French Red Cross). The other honourees depicted in this series are Bernard Palissy (1510–90), Quentin de La Tour (1704–88), Félicité Robert de Lamennais (1782–1854), George Sand (1804–76) and Jules Guesde (1845–1922). This context suggests Joinville was included as a writer, for his contribution to the arts.

Figure 6.5 Joinville 1224–1317, 1957, France. Drawn by Maurice Lalau and engraved by Robert Cami. © *La Poste*, 2017. From author's personal collection. Used by kind permission of *La Poste*.

There is no crusade-specific imagery on Joinville's stamp – the image consists of an artistic portrait in semi-profile. However, Joinville's chronicle, strictly speaking a biography of King Louis IX of France titled the *Life of Saint Louis*, is the principal Western narrative source for the Seventh Crusade, and Joinville's only known work. It is this which makes it crusade specific, as the author simply cannot be divorced from the subject matter.

Two years later, in 1959, Geoffrey de Villehardouin (c. 1150–c. 1213–18), the author of a chronicle of the Fourth Crusade, *De la Conquête de Constantinople* ('On the Conquest of Constantinople'), was featured on a stamp (Figure 6.6). This issue formed a set of six, also titled *Célébrités*. This stamp provides more information to the observer about the context of the honouree, via the background illustrations. Villehardouin is flanked by ships on his left, bearing the image of a cross on their sails. It is a common supposition that crusade ships were decorated in this way, and as such, more firmly communicates the crusade association with the observer. The ships approach a small tower, likely intended to represent Constantinople, and suggesting their purpose is a siege. Over Villehardouin's right shoulder are banners adorned with a cross, in front of pikes and spears. Thus, the military aspect of the crusades is depicted for the first time on a French stamp, but subtly. Similar to that of Joinville, this stamp is a semi-postal, with a surcharge for *Croix-Rouge français*. Considering the small number of crusade-specific issues, the use of a second French crusade-specific image in association with charity fundraising is significant. It speaks

Figure 6.6 Geoffroi de Villehardouin, 1150–1212, 1959, France. Designed by Albert Decaris and engraved by René Cottet. © *La Poste*, 2017. © ADAGP, Paris and DACS, London 2018. From author's personal collection. Used by kind permission of *La Poste*, ADAGP and DACS.

to a desire to interpret the crusades in a charitable context – not belying their military nature, but perhaps seeking to soften it by focusing on aspects such as mutual support.

In 1967, a stamp depicting St. Louis IX was issued. The stamp shows the king sat beneath a tree, receiving the poor. It was accompanied, however, by a Parisian First Day of Issue handstamp, which is crusade specific. It shows the portrait of the king, arrayed for battle, dressed in a mail coif over which he wears his crown, armour and a tunic; on the latter, the top of a cross is just visible. The principal military campaigns of Louis IX were the Seventh and Eighth Crusades; thus, this image is a subtle example of French involvement in the crusades being communicated, accepted and normalised. The stamps were released during the 'politics of grandeur' pursued by President Charles de Gaulle (1890–1970) during the 1960s. This stamp was a component in a multi-part series of stamps on the history of France, featuring past kings, and could thus be associated with a conscious aim of inspiring support at home for de Gaulle's vision of the future of France by recalling the glory of its past and advertising the same to an international audience.

Thereafter, although crusade-related images can be identified, there is a hiatus in crusade-specific imagery until 1998. The absence suggests an increased reticence to philatelically commemorate crusading history through these decades. On 27 April 1998, a single stamp was issued, although it formed part of a series of four featuring the work of famous

Figure 6.7 Delacroix 1798–1863, 1998, France. Layout by Aurélie Baras and engraved by Pierre Albuisson. © *La Poste*, 2017. From author's personal collection. Used by kind permission of *La Poste*, Aurélie Barras and Pierre Albuisson.

artists, released individually throughout the year. The stamp features an extract from the painting *Entrée des croisés à Constantinople* ('The Entry of the Crusaders into Constantinople') by Romantic artist Eugene Delacroix (1798–1863), completed in 1840 (Figure 6.7). It may have been impractical to put the full image on a stamp due to the size of the painting; however, the other three stamps show the works of Paul Gaugin 1848–1903), Pablo Picasso (1881–1973) and Marcel Duchamp (1887–1968) in full. This painting by Delacroix was commissioned by King Louis Philippe (1773–1850), to hang in the *Salles des Croisades* ('Rooms of the Crusades') in the Palace of Versailles, which ultimately comprised five rooms hung with over 120 paintings.[32] Such circumstances suggest that the work was intended to be a celebration of crusading heritage.

However, the impression is not one of triumphant crusaders, but one of human suffering; titular protagonists are cast in shadow in the centre of the picture, whilst attention is drawn to the characters in the foreground, Greek residents of the city. The catalogue in the Louvre (where the painting was transferred in 1885) describes them thus: 'stricken families bar their [the crusaders] way to beg for mercy'.[33] A commentator describes the foreground as one of 'misery, fear and death. A world collapses. Another is born'.[34] Contemporary art critic and Delacroix aficionado Charles Baudelaire (1821–67) in his *Salon de 1846* commented that in several of Delacroix's works, 'you will find a figure which is more stricken, more crushed than the others; a figure in which all the surrounding anguish is epitomized'[35] – his example was the character selected to a feature on this stamp: a woman, her back exposed to the viewer, hair thrown forwards, cradling the body of a dead or unconscious woman in her arms. It is of a person who appears detached, absorbed in grief even in the face of the advancing army. Philatelically, the choice of this work of Delacroix, and a partial selection which focuses on the resultant human loss, represents a conscious decision and a noteworthy shift in emphasis in representations of the crusades.

This is also suggested by the selection in 2001 of a mural from the Knights Hospitaller site, Hôtel des Chevaliers de Saint-Jean de Jérusalem in Toulouse (Figure 6.8). The murals date to the twelfth century, and the image is a particularly famous one, depicting an angel and St. James. As in the 1998 stamp, the primary purpose is promotion of French heritage, and secondarily of religion. However, the use of this image also informs the perception of the crusades – the government was not reluctant to use images from a Military Order in their philatelic advertisements. The name Knights Hospitaller suggests an altruistic and caring affect, focussing on hospital and welfare work. Viewed alongside the 1998 stamp, it seems that during these years, the crusades were being communicated primarily in terms of their human impact and care efforts.

Whilst they fall outside the time frame in which the French government had authority over the images used philatelically, the crusade-specific stamp issues of 2010 to 2017 are also worth noting, as they appear to evidence a further shift in emphasis to a more overt acknowledgement of the military nature of the crusades. In 2012, a series of six stamps titled *Les soldats de plomb* ('lead soldiers') was issued,

Figure 6.8 Hôtel des Chevaliers de Saint-Jean de Jerusalem, 2001, France. Designed and engraved by André Lavergne. © *La Poste*, 2017. From author's personal collection. Used by kind permission of *La Poste* and André Lavergne.

according to the official literature of La Poste, in commemoration of this type of children's toy. One of the stamps is a twelfth-century crusader, arrayed for battle, with spear and shield, and a sword in the background (Figure 6.9). The following year, an issue from the long (multi-year) series, *Les grandes heures de l'Histoire de France* ('greatest hours in the history of France'), depicts the Battle of Muret, key in the Albigensian Crusade (Figure 6.10). These stamps change focus to the soldier and battle.

Figure 6.9 Les soldats de plomb, Croise XIIeme siècle, 2012, France. Designed by Pierre-André Cousin and engraved by Yves Beaujard. © *La Poste*, 2017. From author's personal collection. Used by kind permission of *La Poste*, Pierre-André Cousin and Yves Beaujard.

Figure 6.10 Les grandes heures de l'histoire de France: Muret, 2013, France. Designed and engraved by Louis Boursier. © *La Poste*, 2017. From author's personal collection. Used by kind permission of *La Poste* and Louis Boursier.

Conclusion

Although there is no metric for measuring the impact of stamps and the success of their propaganda, the twentieth century saw extensive use of the postal service and an explosion in stamp design and issues. Prior to the privatisation of a country's postal service, the philatelic issues can be said to be official government documents and thus convey a message to the national and international community about the nature of the issuing country. Broadly speaking, across worldwide stamp issues which bear the word, either by itself or alongside medievalised images of crusaders, the term 'crusade' is employed in a secular context, meaning a campaign for change against a societal enemy. It is a term of significant familiarity to warrant use in identical contexts in stamp issues across Europe and by countries with no direct historical association with the medieval crusades.

A study of French postage stamps has generated an impression of a country which has chosen to depict the medieval crusades philatelically, demonstrating a positive acceptance of the crusades as an element of the nation's history. The number of issues and commemorations is small, compared with the total philatelic output of the country, which suggests a low-key and subtle celebration. It is possible to trace an evolution of national memory of the crusades through the stamps of the twentieth and early twenty-first centuries. The images from the 1950s and 1960s celebrate individuals for their contribution to the cultural history of France. Those from 1998 and 2001 shift emphasis to the human cost of the crusades; however, this message is a secondary one. Those from the early twenty-first century, in contrast, focus on soldiers and battles. Thus, the French interpretation of the crusades aspect of national history, as depicted on postage stamps through these decades, is one of particular, and changing, nuance. As we have seen, postage stamps provide a window into a material memory of the crusades and the ways in which they were memorialised, and their provision of a historical background to the everyday lives of those who used them.

Notes

1 'Universal Postal Convention and Regulations', in *Convention Manual*, Universal Postal Union (Berne, 2018), vol. 1, section 1, Article 6; 3.1; 3.2 and 5 (also n. 1), pp. 8–9.
2 Carlos Stoetzer, *Postage Stamps as Propaganda* (Washington, DC, 1953).
3 Pauliina Raento and Stanley D. Brunn, 'Visualising Finland: Postage Stamps as Political Messengers', *Geografiska Annaler* 87B:(2) (2005), p. 145.

4 Jonathan Phillips, *Holy Warriors: A Modern History of the Crusades* (London, 2009), p. 334.

5 Derek Richardson, *Tables of French Postal Rates 1849 to 2005*, 3rd edn. (Bristol, 2006), p. 4.

6 Jean-Pierre Bertin-Maghit, *Propaganda Documentaries in France 1940–1944*, Trans. Marcelline Block (London, 2016), p. 66.

7 Ibid. p. 71.

8 Ibid.

9 David Stahel, *Operation Barbarossa and Germany's Defeat in the East* (Cambridge, 2009), p. 357.

10 Ibid. p. 40, n. 33.

11 David Stahel ed., *Joining Hitler's Crusade: European Nations and the Invasion of the Soviet Union, 1941* (Cambridge, 2018), pp. 5–7.

12 Jack Child, *Miniature Messages: The Semiotics and Politics of Latin American Postage Stamps* (Durham, 2008), p. 112.

13 Luis C. Cano Guitart, 'El Estado de Necesidad y el sello benéfico', *Historia Postal de Huelva y su Provincia durante la Guerra Civil. La memoria histórica de una correspondencia diferente* (Huelva, 2009), p. 36, <www.filatelia-numismatica.com/articulos/guerracivil/>, [accessed 28 August 2018].

14 Caroline Brothers, *War and Photography: A Cultural History* (London, 2013), pp. 64–5; Phillips, *Holy Warriors*, pp. 323–5.

15 Ibid., p. 325.

16 Ibid.

17 Summarised in Sigard Adolphus Knopf, *A History of the National Tuberculosis Association: The Anti-Tuberculosis Movement in the United States* (New York, 1922), p. 152.

18 E.g., 'Cross of Lorraine', *Breathe: The Lung Association*, <https://nf.lung.ca/about-us/our-history/cross-lorraine>, [accessed 1 September 2018]. Unsupported by published records of the 1902 conference.

19 Pannwitz, *Die Erste Internationale Tuberkulose-Konferenz, Berlin, 22–26 Oct. 1902* (Berlin 1903), pp. 118–120.

20 Noel Cox, 'The Acquisition of Sovereignty by Quasi-States: The Case of the Order of Malta', *Mountbatten Journal of Legal Studies* 6 (2002), pp. 26–47, esp. p. 42.

21 Ibid. p. 43.

22 'Stamps & Coins', *Sovereign Order of Malta*, <https://web.archive.org/web/20190204164907/https://www.orderofmalta.int/stamps/>, [accessed 4 February 2019].

23 See table 'Les timbres par années', Phil-Ouest, 'Les timbres de France', <http://www.phil-ouest.com/Timbres.php>, [accessed 9 February 2019].

24 A Pilgrim, 'The Walsingham Cross', *Life of the Spirit (1946–1964)*, 2:16 (1947), p. 168.

25 Pope Pius XII, 'Christmas Message 1942', *The Internal Order of States and People*, Eternal Word Television Network, <https://www.ewtn.com/library/PAPALDOC/P12CH42.HTM>, [accessed 3 September 2018].

26 Anon., 'Pilgrims of 14 Lands Hear Appeal for Unity', *The Denver Catholic Register* (1 August 1946), p. 8, <https://archives.archden.org/islandora/object/archden%3A7561/datastream/OBJ/view >, [accessed 23 September 2018].

27 Ibid.; A Staff Reporter, 'Vezelay May Become International Centre', *Catholic Herald* (2 August 1946), <http://archive-uat.catholicherald.co.uk/article/2nd-august-1946/1/vezelay-may-become-international-centre>, [accessed 3 September 2018].

28 Philip Nord, 'Catholic Culture in Interwar France', *French Politics, Culture & Society* 21:3 (2003), pp. 6–8.

29 Gerald Vann, 'Pilgrimage for World Peace', *Catholic Herald*, 24 May 1946, <http://archive-uat.catholicherald.co.uk/article/24th-may-1946/2/letters>, [accessed 3 September 2018].

30 'Historical Background', *The Vézelay basilica*, <http://thevezelaybasilica.e-monsite.com/pages/historical-background.html>, [accessed 3 September 2018].

31 Nord, 'Catholic Culture', pp. 5–7. For an English parallel in the form of the Most Noble Order of Crusaders, see Horswell, *British Crusader Medievalism*, pp. 158–82.

32 Jonathan Riley-Smith, *The Crusades, Christianity, and Islam*, (New York, 2011), p. 54; Phillips, *Holy Warriors*, p. 319.

33 Maximilien Gauthier, *Delacroix*, (London, 1964), plate XXV (unnumbered page).

34 Ibid.

35 Charles Baudelaire, *Art in Paris 1845–1862: Salons and Other Exhibitions Reviewed by Charles Baudelaire*, Trans. and ed. Jonathan Mayne (Oxford, 1981), p. 65.

Bibliography

Primary

Anon. 'Pilgrims of 14 Lands Hear Appeal for Unity'. *The Denver Catholic Register* (1 August 1946), p. 8. https://archives.archden.org/islandora/object/archden%3A7561/datastream/OBJ/view. [Accessed 23 September 2018].

Baudelaire, Charles. *Art in Paris 1845–1862. Salons and other Exhibitions Reviewed by Charles Baudelaire*. Trans. & ed. Jonathan Mayne. Oxford: Phaidon, 1981.

A Pilgrim. 'The Walsingham Cross'. *Life of the Spirit (1946–1964)* 2:16 (1947), pp. 167–71.

Pope Pius XII. 'Christmas Message 1942'. *The Internal Order of States and People*. Eternal Word Television Network, www.ewtn.com/library/PAPALDOC/P12CH42.HTM. [Accessed 3 September 2018].

Pannwitz. *Die Erste Internationale Tuberkulose-Konferenz, Berlin, 22–26 Oct. 1902*. Berlin: Internationalaes Central-Bureau zur Bekampfung der Tuberkulose, 1903.

Phil-Ouest, 'Les timbres de France'. http://www.phil-ouest.com/Timbres.php. [Accessed 9 February 2019].

Sovereign Order of Malta. 'Stamps & Coins'. https://web.archive.org/web/20190204164907/https://www.orderofmalta.int/stamps/ [Accessed 4 February 2019].

A Staff Reporter. 'Vezelay May Become International Centre'. *Catholic Herald* (2August1946).http://archive-uat.catholicherald.co.uk/article/2nd-august-1946/1/vezelay-may-become-international-centre. [Accessed 3 September 2018].

Universal Postal Union. *Convention Manual.* Berne: International Bureau of the Universal Postal Union, 2018.

Vann, Gerald. 'Pilgrimage for World Peace'. *Catholic Herald* (24 May 1946). http://archive-uat.catholicherald.co.uk/article/24th-may-1946/2/letters. [Accessed 3 September 2018].

Secondary

Bertin-Maghit, Jean-Pierre. *Propaganda Documentaries in France 1940–1944.* Trans. Marcelline Block. Lanham, Boulder, New York, London: Rowman & Littlefield, 2016.

Breathe: The Lung Association. 'Cross of Lorraine'. https://nf.lung.ca/about-us/our-history/cross-lorraine. [Accessed 1 September 2018].

Brothers, Caroline. *War and Photography: A Cultural History.* London & New York: Routledge, 2013.

Cano Guitart, Luis Carlos. 'El Estado de Necesidad y el sello benéfico'. *Historia Postal de Huelva y su Provincia durante la Guerra Civil. La memoria histórica de una correspondencia diferente.* Huelva: Filatelia-Numismática San José, 2009. www.filatelia-numismatica.com/articulos/guerracivil/. [Accessed 28 August 2018].

Child, Jack. *Miniature Messages: The Semiotics and Politics of Latin American Postage Stamps.* Durham: Duke University Press, 2008.

Cox, Noel. 'The Acquisition of Sovereignty by Quasi-States: The case of the Order of Malta'. *Mountbatten Journal of Legal Studies* 6:1–2 (2002), pp. 26–47.

Gauthier, Maximilien. *Delacroix.* London: Oldbourne Press, 1964.

Horswell, Mike. *The Rise and Fall of British Crusader Medievalism, c. 1825–1945.* Abingdon: Routledge, 2018.

Knopf, Sigard Adolphus. *A History of the National Tuberculosis Association: The Anti-Tuberculosis Movement in the United States.* New York City: National Tuberculosis Association, 1922.

Nord, Philip. 'Catholic Culture in Interwar France'. *French Politics Culture & Society* 21:3 (2003), pp. 1–20.

Phillips, Jonathan. *Holy Warriors: A Modern History of the Crusades.* London: Vintage Books, 2009.

Raento, Pauliina, and Stanley D. Brunn. 'Visualising Finland: Postage Stamps as Political Messengers'. *Geografiska Annaler* 87B:(2) (2005), pp. 145–63.

Richardson, Derek. *Tables of French Postal Rates 1849 to 2005*, 3rd Edition. Bristol: France & Colonies Philatelic Society of Great Britain, 2006.

Riley-Smith, Jonathan. *The Crusades, Christianity, and Islam.* New York: Columbia University Press, 2011.

Stahel, David. *Operation Barbarossa and Germany's Defeat in the East.* Cambridge: Cambridge University Press, 2009.

Stahel, David, ed. *Joining Hitler's Crusade: European Nations and the Invasion of the Soviet Union, 1941.* Cambridge: Cambridge University Press, 2018.

Stoetzer, Carlos. *Postage Stamps as Propaganda.* Washington, DC: Public Affairs Press, 1953.

The Vézelay basilica. 'Historical Background'. http://thevezelaybasilica.e-monsite.com/pages/historical-background.html. [Accessed 3 September 2018].

7   Wikipedia and the crusades

Constructing and communicating crusading

Mike Horswell

Introduction: crusading 'WikiKnowledge'

In April 2005, one Wikipedia contributor glibly described the crusades as 'a bit of a sleepy topic actually'. Almost immediately a heated discussion occupied the 'Talk' discussion pages for the rest of the month on the nature of the crusades and their relevance for the present, provoked by the 'War on Terror' being described as a 'Tenth Crusade' and suggestions that it thus merited mention on the 'Crusades' page. 'All that matters is that people are talking about a Tenth Crusade, not just a couple of people but millions of people, it's a current concept!', argued 'Mgekelly'. The original contributor responded: 'The War on Terror is a current event – let the historians of the distant future decide if there was continuity between the crusades of nearly a millenium [sic] ago, and the War on Terror in the present day'. They later added, 'Playing with History – much like Fire, is Dangerous [...] "Crusade" isn't just some amorphous blob we can apply to any war we feel like!'[1]

Wikipedia articles increasingly set the tone for popular perceptions of a topic. The online, freely accessible and editable encyclopaedia birthed in 2001 is rated as one of the most visited sites on the Internet.[2] According to Wikimedia's statistics, the English-language Wikipedia garnered 7.48 billion page views in November 2018 and 92.04 billion in the year 2018.[3] Summaries of Wikipedia articles appear in Google Search results and are linked to by Facebook and YouTube as 'fact checking' standards, whilst Wikipedia is a reference point for in-home digital assistants and search engines.[4] It is also used in universities by students and staff alike, despite a traditional scepticism of its value.[5] 'Wikipedia', Heather Ford has argued:

> is important because it has become entangled in our everyday lives. Because of its ubiquity, ease of use and centrality to the Web experience, Wikipedia has become a marker of importance, a symbol of notability, a site of information power.[6]

Playing with fire may be an overblown analogy for writing history but as this volume and other recent work has shown perceptions of the crusades and crusading remain potent. The pages of Wikipedia on the crusades represent a productive place for the study of crusader medievalism – how the crusades are remembered and used. They stand at an intersection of academic knowledge and popular perceptions of the medieval expeditions, providing a site for the encounter of crosscurrents of historical interpretation. However, these interactions are structured by Wikipedia's nature – its policies, culture and material limitations – which determine what I am designating 'Wiki-Knowledge', the type of information available from Wikipedia. In turn, Wikipedia actively generates a globally influential version of crusading history; perhaps the *most* influential.

Unlike conventional encyclopaedias or traditional publications, Wikipedia articles are freely and collaboratively editable, and both benefit and suffer from the resultant fluidity. Articles are structurally open to defacing and manipulation, though also easily revised and corrected; criticism can be negated with a few quick edits. They are always in flux, subject to 'perpetual revision or reconstruction'.[7] In practice, there is an uneven distribution of the quality (variously measured) of articles,[8] whilst structural features (such as policies, requirements of technical literacy, and lack of diversity amongst contributors) determine the types of knowledge created (or at least, kept).[9] For example, the 'Neutral Point of View' (NPOV) policy requires a 'neutral' stance throughout and reference to 'verifiable' external sources rather than the original research of contributors. This 'circumscribes the boundaries of what counts as knowledge on Wikipedia' and structures both articles and discussions of topics.[10] NPOV 'underscores, rather than resolves, the fundamental problem of social knowledge production' in that it brings to the fore questions of what counts as 'verifiable' and 'neutral' and who decides.[11]

Despite this, studies suggest that Wikipedia stands up well on grounds of reliability, in terms of accuracy, breadth and depth of coverage, and readability, and unsurprisingly outstrips its competitors when it comes to 'currency' ('up-to-dateness').[12] There is significant variation across content: 'While some articles are of the highest quality of scholarship, others are admittedly complete rubbish'.[13] Wikipedia articles must be considered, and read, *as an encyclopaedia*, 'with all the limitations that entails' an older version of the same article argued; Don Fallis has suggested that Wikipedia should more appropriately be compared with online, freely accessible alternatives, such as blogs, ultimately to Wikipedia's advantage.[14]

Wikipedia has always been more than its articles, each of which comes with a complete revision history of all edits made and 'Talk' page for discussion of the construction and modification of the article. These two features render visible the processes of article-creation: they 'show the construction of a significant objectified social reality' and reveal 'the textual mediation of social reality'.[15] Moreover, they are a key arena for study of Wikipedia knowledge-creation beyond their 'real-time', 'behind-the-scenes' value – the 'Talk' pages 'are at the cutting edge of social legitimation, since they reveal the on-going process of both apprehending and producing the realities of [the article's content]'.[16] In other words, Wikipedia reflects the state and history of popular knowledge as well as creating it: Wikipedia has a 'paradoxical stature as both *record* and *source* of information'.[17]

Constructing the crusades

Given the above, what is the version of crusading and the crusades presented by Wikipedia? This chapter presents a necessarily limited sketch of crusading 'WikiKnowledge' and is concerned with mapping two topographies: the epistemological dimensions of Wikipedia's 'Crusades' article and 'Talk' pages and the ethnographic geography of the community engaged in their creation. The first aspect involves tracing the terrain of knowledge presented, its production, and relationship to academic discourse on the crusades. Constraints of space prevent a comprehensive evaluation of all references to the crusades and crusading on Wikipedia, or even of all articles on relevant topics. I will focus on the 'Crusades' article as it is the 'landing page' for anyone searching for the crusades in general, and, in part because of this, it reflects the most direct engagement of editors with crusading and the crusades.[18] The fluid nature of Wikipedia articles means that to an extent any analysis of content is instantly outdated; specific criticisms made here can be addressed by editors of the articles in the future and thus nullified.[19] This evaluation, therefore, pertains to the 'Crusades' article as it appeared on 30 November 2018 and to discussions of the article in its related archive of 'Talk' pages.[20] Together, the article and 'Talk' forum facilitate the use of methods developed by online ethnography studies to address the second aspect of the 'WikiKnowledge' of the crusades considered here. They reveal the shape of the social landscape of an online community of Wikipedia contributors, which frames the social context of its production.[21] In short, they enable us to see a snapshot of how the crusades are presented and how that image was arrived at.

Crusading on Wikipedia consists of an overview article on the historical crusades ('Crusades') as well as articles covering subtopics in detail. The scope is set out in several places which present a broad approach to crusading as popular and non-Levantine campaigns are included.[22] The 'Crusades' article has seven categories and is roughly 12,450 words long.[23] It covers the terminology of crusading, the historical background of the Eastern Mediterranean, campaigns from the eleventh to fifteenth centuries, the crusader states, the military orders, the legacy of the crusades and their historiography. This range, and its organisation, reflects an understanding of crusading requiring appreciation of the pre-1095 context in order to see what was 'new' in Pope Urban II's call at Clermont. It is a 'pluralist' view, which includes crusades against Christians and pagans, Baltic campaigns and the Iberian '*Reconquista*'.

The crusades, the article begins, were 'a series of religious wars sanctioned by the Latin Church in the medieval period'.[24] Primarily aimed at the reconquest of 'the Holy Land from Muslim rule', the term crusade 'is also applied to other church-sanctioned campaigns [...] fought for a variety of reasons including the suppression of paganism and heresy, the resolution of conflict among rival Roman Catholic groups, or for political and territorial advantage'. The most notable absence from this definition is the classic formulation of Jonathan Riley-Smith, repeated in many of his works, that the crusades were 'penitential war-pilgrimages'[25]: indeed, 'The defining, and most radical, feature of a crusade was that it was penitential.'[26] Riley-Smith's emphasis has not been without criticism, but has found many adherents and foregrounds the role of the papacy which the Wikipedia article repeats ('church-sanctioned').[27] His linkage of 'pilgrimage' with crusading has resonated with crusade historians, not least as the language of the former had been adopted by those who participated in, and described, the medieval crusades.[28] The definition of a crusade, or crusading, has proven a thorny issue for crusade historians in a historiographical debate reported by the article in the 'Terminology' section.[29] The lack of clarity in definition has stimulated investigation into what has been perceived as crusading, not least as scholarship has looked beyond the traditional focus of the subject, namely, the nine-numbered expeditions and crusader states in the Levant.[30]

In parallel with the historians, the editors and contributors to the Wikipedia article grappled with the same question, though within different parameters. Key questions in the historical debate have included the novelty of Urban's synthesis of ideas, the centrality of the Holy Land, the role of the papacy, the significance of ecclesiastical apparatus, the language of crusading and the motivations of crusaders.[31] These debates are reflected in the article's 'Talk' pages: for example, suggestions are repeatedly made to limit its scope to the numbered expeditions or crusades to the Middle East.[32]

In the same vein, editors and historians alike have wrestled with the framing of the crusades as a defensive war. Historian Paul Crawford has made the case for the crusades as a retaliation for seventh-century–Islamic conquests and in defence of a Western European Christendom, whilst Kristin Skottki has suggested that this argument is based on acceptance of medieval Christian propaganda, which uncritically accepts a 'Clash of Civilisations' model of Christian-Muslim interaction.[33] Wikipedia editors too debated the subject, though within the bounds of the encyclopaedia's policies. The question of whether characterising the crusades as 'defensive' inherently implied a particular point of view (in contravention of NPOV) was considered alongside relevant historical considerations.[34]

Rather than making a binding decision on the issue, the editors attempted to reflect the state of academic discussion and represent differing viewpoints. This inevitably led to the question of *which* sources should be selected as representative. Thomas Madden's advocacy of the crusades-as-defensive position in popular and academic works was considered:

> The defensive/offensive thing is actually pretty important and we shouldn't really leave it out [...] whatever your opinion of Madden's politics, he is nevertheless an influential and respected crusade scholar, and his views are among those that should be represented here.[35]

Agreement was reached that scholarly works of respected crusades historians should be cited rather than their non-scholarly interventions.[36] Here, the community of Wikipedia editors and contributors could be seen engaging with a historical debate about the nature of crusading, albeit within particular constraints on both form and content: their article was required to be 'neutral' and reflective of 'academic' concerns, adhering to NPOV, which directly shaped the article's presentation of crusading.

Other tensions in the presentation of the crusade were caused, or ameliorated, by the specifics of Wikipedia's formatting and history. Originally titled 'Crusade', after discussion the editors added an 's' to the article's title in September 2006 in order to distinguish the content as the history of the medieval expeditions rather than 'the concept of

crusade', or crusading.[37] This, along with the creation of a 'Historiography of the Crusades' page, absorbed most of the attempts to add
sections addressing the modern resonance or perceived continuation
of the crusades – a persistent problem. For example, a 'Tenth Crusade'
kept being inserted into the article describing the twenty-first–century
U.S.-led invasion of Iraq and the 'War on Terror', whilst the 'Talk'
pages reveal several lengthy discussions, asserting that without this
the article represented a Western 'Euro-centric' perspective.[38] These
were largely the suggestions of passing contributors, representing a
topical concern perhaps, and were often opposed by longer term contributors to, or editors of, the article. The article's dry opening remark
under 'Terminology' represents some of the fatigue editors share with
crusade historians at attempts to narrow or broaden definitions:

> The term *crusade* used in modern historiography at first referred
> to the wars in the Holy Land beginning in 1095, but the range of
> events to which the term has been applied has been greatly ex-
> tended, so that its use can create a misleading impression of coher-
> ence, particularly regarding the early Crusades.[39]

The approach of shunting this material into a separate article repeats
the process identified by René König with regard to arguments that
overwhelmed the capacity of article editors to manage the debate
through other means: 'the community reacts to this overload by mar-
ginalizing alternative interpretations and immunizing the article from
them'.[40]

Verifying the crusades

Large sections of the article depend on Thomas Asbridge's *The
Crusades* (2010) and Peter Lock's *Routledge Companion to the Crusades*
(2006).[41] Asbridge provides much of the material for eleventh- and
twelfth-century crusading, whilst Lock's work is used for broader
arenas of crusading activity. In general, the sources are deployed
effectively. Robert Chazan's *European Jewry and the First Crusade*
(1996) is cited when the pogroms in the Rhineland on the First Crusade are mentioned and the millenarianism of poor participants in
the same expedition merited reference to Norman Cohn's *The Pursuit
of the Millennium* (1970), though Jay Rubenstein's *Armies of Heaven*
(2011) is a notable omission.[42]

There are some signs of fraying, however. Standard overview works
on the Fourth Crusade by Jonathan Phillips, Donald Queller and

Thomas Madden are missing, despite appearing on the 'Fourth Crusade' page, and Erik Christiansen's work on the Northern, or Baltic, Crusades is also absent.[43] On the other hand, the 'Crusades' article collects a number of minor, or tangentially related, sources. Some of these are from broad surveys – appropriate to reference for an encyclopaedia – but others are narrowly focussed articles out of place in an overview.[44] There is potential here for authorial self-promotion, as encouraged by some publishers' marketing advice. The uneven handling of sources is illustrated by the repetition of a phrase from Norman Davies' *Europe* (1997) three times in which he argued that the crusades 'strengthen[ed] the nexus between Western Christendom, feudalism, and militarism'.[45] Whilst feudalism is a disputed term, it is here parsed uncritically. More contentiously, the article asserts that 'The Kingdom of Jerusalem was the first experiment in European colonialism creating a "Europe Overseas" or Outremer', and quotes Davies again. Davies, in fact, omitted 'European colonialism' – a seemingly minor difference but one which refused to locate the crusades as an originary point for later imperialism. The relationship between colonialism and the crusades, especially in the form of the crusader states, has exercised historians who have debated the utility of employing terms such as 'colony' and 'apartheid' for medieval phenomena.[46] Moreover, the association between crusading and colonialism is fraught for modern audiences.

The lack of coherence with regard to sources used, vision of the crusades and written style are features of the article's construction. The article has had 10,391 edits and 4,028 editors since its creation in October 2001; the top 10 per cent of editors have made 19.5 per cent of the edits.[47] Presently, 55.3 per cent of the article's text can be attributed (by characters edited) to one editor, 'Norfolkbigfish', who is also the top editor by number of edits to the article in total.[48] Very little, if any, of the original text imported from the *New Schaff-Herzog Encyclopedia of Religious Knowledge* (1909) remains.[49] Analysis of when the article was edited, and its variations in size, demonstrates that it received increasing attention from 2004 to 2007, when editing peaked with over 300 edits each month between January and May (Figure 7.1).[50] Notable spurts of change in the past five years (around 100 edits in a month) were April and May 2013, September 2015, June and July 2016, and December 2016 to March 2017.

The fragmentary nature of the article's creation and the competition of voices it embodies are a direct consequence of Wikipedia's policies on open co-authorship, NPOV, and 'Notability'. The latter policy requires authors to reflect academic scholarship, in the spirit of

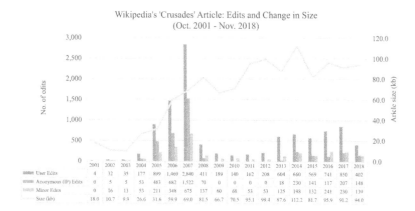

Figure 7.1 Wikipedia's 'Crusades' Article: Edits and Change in Size (October 2001 to November 2018). Data from 'Crusades: en. wikipedia.org', *xTools*.

an encyclopaedia, rather than conduct and write 'original research'. Consequentially, the article is often both outdated, as cutting-edge scholarship is often less accessible to non-academics, yet able to incorporate articles as they are published if editors do have access.[51] Given these constraints, and the potential for vandalism from a multitude of sources, the level of coherence and accuracy of the 'Crusades' article is impressive, when read as an encyclopaedia article.

Communicating crusading

Establishing reception, or cultural impact, is notoriously difficult. In the case of traditional printed encyclopaedias, for example, sales figures, library acquisition and borrowing records, and (possibly) other oblique references might be all we have to establish the readership and influence of a particular work, let alone of a specific article.[52] In contrast, the English-language Wikipedia article on the crusades had 6.74 million views by users between July 2015 and November 2018 and averaged nearly 5,400 views a day.[53] For the same period, Figure 7.2 shows the pageviews of users of the 'Crusades' article alongside selected related articles, indicating their relative popularity and its volatility.[54] The examples here were chosen for comparison and because they illustrate distinct spikes in numbers at particular times, a provocation for further research. What, for example, explains the November 2015 peak in pageviews of the 'Crusades' page? Is the December 2017

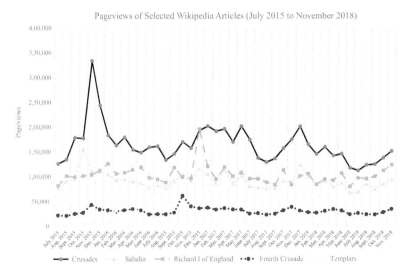

Figure 7.2 Pageviews of Selected Wikipedia Articles (July 2015 to November 2018). Data from 'Pageviews', *Wikimedia*.

jump in pageviews for the 'Templars' article due to the release of the TV series *Knightfall*?[55] What about the February to May 2016 interest in the same article?

Although these statistics do not present the level of engagement indicated by each pageview, if even a small fraction do represent a deep engagement with the content presented by the articles, then they demonstrate significant communication of a particular perception of the crusades. If the figures presented above for user edits are taken as an index of deep engagement with the ideas of crusading, combined with those who contributed to, or read, the 'Talk:Crusades' archives, there is clearly a substantial community of those interested in the crusades gathered around the Wikipedia pages. Indeed, the 'Talk:Crusades' archives are over 130,000 words long.

Conclusion

The 'Crusades' article bears the marks of its patchwork creation. It is up to date in areas, yet missing standard works in others; clear in overview and scope of the subject, but dependent on single works for large sections; and hardest to combat for a multi-authored piece of this length, uneven in tone and consistency of presentation of crusading.

More surprisingly perhaps, the article remains informative, broad in coverage, clearly signposts academic work and related topics, and includes works published in 2018. The 'Talk' pages demonstrate how contributors have wrestled with some of the same questions which have vexed historians, whilst being unable to ignore ones generated by popular perceptions (and misconceptions) of crusading and the crusades.

The 'Crusades' article – as can be seen through the number of pageviews, edits and contributions to the 'Talk' pages – is a significant site of public grappling with the history and meaning of the crusades. If it reflects traditional (academic) perceptions of the crusades this is because it is both designed to and because a number of editors have chosen to interpret, enact and enforce the policies of NPOV and 'Notability'.[56] Deficiency or disparity of source coverage could be due in part to their inaccessibility; whether articles being behind paywalls or few contributors having access to the range of monograph studies of crusading written by a crusade scholar. That out-of-copyright sources are often accessible online, and therefore disproportionately represented in Wikipedia, leads to the revival of outmoded historical assessments; the resurrection, zombie-like, of old interpretations of crusading with their associated baggage.[57]

Wikipedia's representation of knowledge remains paradoxically new, yet old, in other ways. The open access, freely editable nature of Wikipedia has been heralded as radically pointing to a new concept of knowledge itself: 'In today's world, knowledge should be flexible, fallible, refutable, and its quest should involve change, disagreement, and continuous partial revision'.[58] Yet, this could also be a description of the scientific method or academic historiographical processes of knowledge-creation. The difference is that Wikipedia makes these processes visible whilst rendering the types of expertise necessary for proficient knowledge-creation opaque.[59] Coupled with its reach, Wikipedia's recording of the complete history of edits and accompanying discussions of edited topics renders it an invaluable – yet underused – source for historians of cultural and collective memories of the past.

This preliminary study is necessarily partial: it has evaluated neither other crusade-related articles (or 'Talk' pages) in the English-language Wikipedia nor those in different languages. But it has been sufficient to highlight the contingent nature of crusading knowledge presented in the 'Crusades' article and some of the structural features of its production. Articles are always in-process, always becoming – their stability is fragile and their content in flux. This chapter has mapped some of the terrain of crusading 'WikiKnowledge', its history, its correspondence with crusade historiography, and its ethnographic context of a community of editors, whilst pointing the way for future studies. As important as Wikipedia is for reflecting and creating knowledge of the crusades and crusading globally, readers must recognise that the perceptions presented are the product of limited, structured consensus. And, 'consensus at Wikipedia', Scott Kildall and Nathaniel Stern remind us, 'is not consensus on a given topic, ready for worldwide dissemination via the site; it is merely a consensus at Wikipedia'.[60]

Notes

1 These quotes from 'Talk:Crusades/Archive 1', *Wikipedia*, <https://en.wikipedia.org/wiki/Talk:Crusades/Archive_1>, [accessed 4 December 2018].

2 Ranked fifth at *alexa.com*, <https://www.alexa.com/topsites>, [accessed 3 December 2018]; eleventh at *similarweb.com*, <https://web.archive.org/web/20181203102832/https://www.similarweb.com/top-websites>, [accessed 3 December 2018]; ninth for domains at 'The Moz Top 500', *moz.com*, <https://web.archive.org/web/20181203110705/https://moz.com/top500>, [accessed 3 December 2018].

3 'Total Page Views, *Wikimedia Statistics*, <https://stats.wikimedia.org/v2/#/en.wikipedia.org/reading/total-page-views/normal||2018-01-01~2019-01-01|~total|>, [accessed 16 May 2019].

4 Noam Cohen, 'Conspiracy Videos? Fake News? Enter Wikipedia, the "Good Cop" of the Internet', *Washington Post Online*, 6 April 2018, <https://web.archive.org/web/20180614045810/https://www.washingtonpost.com/outlook/conspiracy-videos-fake-news-enter-wikipedia-the-good-cop-of-the-internet/2018/04/06/ad1f018a-3835-11e8-8fd2-49fe3c675a89_story.html?utm_term=.1e1ce25a2d95>, [accessed 3 December 2018]; Heather Ford, 'Fact Factories: Wikipedia and the Power to Represent', PhD Thesis (University of Oxford, 2015), pp. 14–17.

5 Charles Knight and Sam Pryke, 'Wikipedia and the University, A Case Study', *Teaching in Higher Education* 17:6 (2012), pp. 649–59.

6 Heather Ford, 'Foreword: Wikipedia and the Sum of All Human Knowledge', *Nordisk Tidsskrift for Informationsvidenskab Og Kulturformidling* 5:1 (2016), p. 9.

7 Peter Burke, *A Social History of Knowledge II: From the Encyclopédie to Wikipedia* (Cambridge, 2012), p. 273.

8 See Mostafa Mesgari et al., '"The Sum of All Human Knowledge": A Systematic Review of Scholarly Research on the Content of Wikipedia', *Journal of the Association for Information Science and Technology* 66:2 (2015), pp. 219–45.

9 Geert Lovink and Nathaniel Tkacz, 'The "C" in CPOV: Introduction to the CPOV Reader', in *CPOV*, pp. 10–11; Heather Ford and R. Stuart Geiger, '"Writing Up Rather than Writing Down": Becoming Wikipedia Literate', in *Proceedings of the Eighth Annual International Symposium on Wikis and Open Collaboration* (Linz, 2012), pp. 1–4; Heather Ford and Judy Wajcman, '"Anyone Can Edit", Not Everyone Does: Wikipedia's Infrastructure and the Gender Gap', *Social Studies of Science* 47:4 (2017), pp. 511–27.

10 Lovink and Tkacz, 'Introduction', pp. 10–11.
11 Lindsay Fullerton and James Ettema, 'Ways of Worldmaking in Wikipedia: Reality, Legitimacy and Collaborative Knowledge Making', *Media, Culture & Society* 36:2 (2014), p. 186.
12 Mesgari et al., 'Review'.
13 'Wikipedia:Ten things you may not know about Wikipedia', *Wikipedia*, <https://en.wikipedia.org/wiki/Wikipedia:Ten_things_you_may_not_know_about_Wikipedia>, [accessed 12 December 2018].
14 Quoted in Joseph Reagle, 'The Argument Engine', in *CPOV*, p. 25; Don Fallis, 'Toward an Epistemology of Wikipedia', *Journal of the American Society for Information Science and Technology* 59:10 (2008), p. 1667.
15 René König, 'Wikipedia', *Information, Communication & Society* 16:2 (2013), p. 164; Fullerton and Ettema, 'Worldmaking', p. 184.
16 Ibid., pp. 197–98.
17 Scott Kildall and Nathaniel Stern, 'Wikipedia Art: Citation as Performative Act', in *CPOV*, p. 170.
18 'Crusades', *Wikipedia*, <https://en.wikipedia.org/wiki/Crusades>, [accessed 30 November 2018]. See also Archives 1–9 at 'Talk:Crusades/Archive index', *Wikipedia*, <https://en.wikipedia.org/wiki/Talk:Crusades/Archive_index>, [accessed 30 November 2018].
19 In the interests of limiting such circularity, it should be noted that I have not edited these pages myself.
20 This version of the page can be seen at 'Wikipedia:Crusades', *Wikipedia*, <https://web.archive.org/web/20181130164144/https://en.wikipedia.org/wiki/Crusades>, [accessed 30 November 2018].
21 Jörgen Skågeby, 'Online Ethnographic Methods: Towards a Qualitative Understanding of Virtual Community Practices', in *Handbook of Research on Methods and Techniques for Studying Virtual Communities: Paradigms and Phenomena*, ed. Ben Kei Daniel (Hershey, PA: IGI Global, 2011), pp. 410–28; Anna Haverinen, 'Internet Ethnography: The Past, the Present and the Future', *Ethnologia Fennica* 42 (2015), pp. 79–90.
22 The 'Crusades' article has a sidebar with links; a 'Portal' page presents an introduction to the crusades (from 'Crusades', *Wikipedia*) and list of related pages ('Portal:Crusades', *Wikipedia*, <https://en.wikipedia.org/wiki/Portal:Crusades>, [accessed 30 November 2018]); and there is an index of crusading subjects ('Category:Crusades', *Wikipedia*, <https://en.wikipedia.org/wiki/Category:Crusades>, [accessed 30 November 2018]).
23 The categories and subheadings are as follows: (1) In the Holy Land (1095–1291): First; 1101; Norwegian; Venetian; Second; Third; 1197; Fourth; Fifth; Sixth; Barons'; Seventh; Eighth; Ninth. (2) After 1291: Smyrniote 1343–1351; Alexandrian 1365; Savoyard 1366; Barbary 1390; Nicopolis 1396; Varna 1443; Portuguese 1481; Spanish 1505–1510. (3) Northern Crusades (1147–1410): Wendish 1147; Swedish 1150; 1249; 1293; Livonian 1198–1290; Prussian 1217–1274; Novgorod 1241–1242; Lithuanian 1283–1410. (4) Popular crusades: People's 1096; Children's 1212; Shepherds' 1251; Poor 1309; Shepherds' 1320. (5) Against Christians: Bosnian 1235–1241; Albigensian 1209–1229; Aragonese 1284/5; Despenser's 1382/3; Hussite 1419–1434. (6) Reconquista (718–1492): Barbastro 1063; Mallorca 1113–1115; Las Navas de Tolosa 1212. (7) Other: Mongol 1241. Each links to separate Wikipedia articles.

24 'Crusades', *Wikipedia.*
25 Jonathan Riley-Smith, *The Crusades: A History*, 3rd edn. (London, 2014), p. 13.
26 Jonathan Riley-Smith, *What Were the Crusades?*, 4th edn. (Basingstoke, 2009), p. 55.
27 'The crusades were papal instruments, the most spectacular expressions of the Papal Monarchy, the armies of the Christian Republic marching in response to calls from the men who on earth represented its monarch.' Riley-Smith, *What Were the Crusades?*, p. 50.
28 Phillips, *Holy Warriors*, p. 4; Tyerman, *Debate*, p. 223. Regarding pilgrimage terminology, the article (accurately) references Thomas Asbridge, *The Crusades: The War for the Holy Land* (London, 2010), p. 40; Christopher Tyerman, *God's War: A New History of the Crusades* (London, 2007), p. 258.
29 See Tyerman, *Debate*, pp. 225 and 233. Tyerman's monograph on academic crusade scholarship is missing from the 'Historiography' section of the article and never referred to – a glaring omission given its focus.
30 Horswell, *British Crusader Medievalism*, p. 13.
31 For a provocative overview, see Christopher Tyerman, *The Invention of the Crusades* (New York, 1998).
32 E.g. December 2006 discussions at 'Talk: Crusades/Archive4', *Wikipedia*, <https://en.wikipedia.org/wiki/Talk:Crusades/Archive_4>, [accessed 5 December 2018].
33 Paul Crawford, 'The First Crusade: Unprovoked Offense or Overdue Defense?', in *Seven Myths of the Crusades*, eds. Alfred J. Andrea and Andrew Holt (Indianapolis, IN, 2015), pp. 1–28; Kristin Skottki, 'The Dead, the Revived and the Recreated Pasts: "Structural Amnesia" in Representations of Crusade History', in *Engaging the Crusades, Volume One*, pp. 120–23.
34 See July 2007 discussion at 'Talk:Crusades/Archive5', *Wikipedia*, <https://en.wikipedia.org/wiki/Talk:Crusades/Archive_5>, [accessed 5 December 2018]. For the policy, see 'Wikipedia:Neutral point of view', *Wikipedia*, <https://en.wikipedia.org/wiki/Wikipedia:Neutral_point_of_view>, [accessed 10 December 2018].
35 'Adam Bishop', 7 July 2007, 'Talk:Crusades/Archive5'. See also 'Norfolkbigfish', 'Madden's views [...] are well known and are referred to the body of the article. They have been much discussed by editors and the current wording is the consensus established. Sourcing is there to his books rather than a magazine article which is unsuitable. It is worth noting that this is a minority view amongst historians; the predominant view is that there are multiple root causes, not purely defensive war.' 8 October 2015, 'Talk:Crusades/Archive9', *Wikipedia*, <https://en.wikipedia.org/wiki/Talk:Crusades/Archive_9>, [accessed 5 December 2018].
36 'Stalwart111' wrote in another discussion of Madden's work, 'the trick here is to find *serious* scholarship from *serious* scholars, not less-serious editorial from serious scholars.' 27 September 2013, 'Talk:Crusades/Archive8', *Wikipedia*, <https://en.wikipedia.org/wiki/Talk:Crusades/Archive_8>, [accessed 5 December 2018]. See 'Wikipedia:Notability', *Wikipedia*, <https://en.wikipedia.org/wiki/Wikipedia:Notability>, [accessed 10 December 2018].
37 'John Kenney', 26 August 2006, discussion at 'Talk: Crusades/Archive3', *Wikipedia*, <https://en.wikipedia.org/wiki/Talk:Crusades/Archive_3>, [accessed 4

124   *Mike Horswell*

December 2018]. See 'Talk:Crusades/Archive4'. The question was first raised by Larry Sanger, co-creator of Wikipedia. 'Talk:Crusades/Archive 1'.

38 Discussions of these insertions occurred in March 2004, February to May 2005; ibid.

39 'Crusades', *Wikipedia.*

40 König, 'Wikipedia', p. 172.

41 Asbridge, *The Crusades*; Peter Lock, *The Routledge Companion to the Crusades* (Abingdon, 2006). There are 51 unique references to Asbridge's work and 31 to Lock's, out of 171.

42 Robert Chazan, *European Jewry and the First Crusade* (Los Angeles, 1996); Norman Cohn, *The Pursuit of the Millennium: Revolutionary Millenarians and Mystical Anarchists of the Middle Ages*, rev. edn. (New York, 1970); Jay Rubenstein, *Armies of Heaven: The First Crusade and the Quest for Apocalypse* (New York, 2011).

43 Jonathan Phillips, *The Fourth Crusade and Sack of Constantinople* (London, 2005); Donald E. Queller and Thomas F. Madden, *The Fourth Crusade: The Conquest of Constantinople*, 2nd edn. (Philadelphia, 1999); Eric Christiansen, *The Northern Crusades*, 2nd edn. (London, 1997).

44 Two examples of the latter appear only in the 'Further Reading' section and are uncited in the body of the text: these are articles by Lucas Villegas-Aristizábal (2018) and Darius Von Güttner Sporzyński (2008).

45 Norman Davies, *Europe: A History* (London, 1997), p. 359. The 'Crusades' article has 'reinforced [or sometimes 'reinforcing'] the connection between Western Christendom, feudalism and militarism.'

46 See Benjamin Z. Kedar et al., 'The Crusading Kingdom of Jerusalem – The First European Colonial Society? A Symposium', in *The Horns of Hattin*, ed. Benjamin Z. Kedar (London, 1987), pp. 341–66; Joshua Prawer, *The Crusaders' Kingdom: European Colonialism in the Middle Ages*, rev. edn. (London, 2001); Ronnie Ellenblum, *Crusader Castles and Modern Histories* (Cambridge, 2007).

47 'Crusades: en.wikipedia.org', *xTools*, <https://xtools.wmflabs.org/articleinfo/en.wikipedia.org/Crusades>, [accessed 7 December 2018].

48 Ibid. The top three users by number of edits are 'Norfolkbigfish', 513 (25.3% of total edits); 'Ealdgyth', 327 (16.1%); and 'Adam Bishop', 276 (13.6%). The top three editors by amount of added words are 'Barbatus', 128,615 (11.2%); 'Ghostexorcist', 88,956 (7.6%); and 'Norfolkbigfish', 77,518 (6.8%).

49 Friedrich Wiegand, 'Crusades', in *The New Schaff-Herzog Encyclopedia of Religious Knowledge*, ed. Samuel Macauley Jackson, (New York, 1909), pp. 315–18.

50 See sections 'Year Counts' and 'Month Counts' at 'Crusades: en.wikipedia. org', *xTools.*

51 For an evaluation of the *Encyclopaedia Britannica*'s articles on the crusades, see Mike Horswell, 'From "Superstitious Veneration" to "War to Defend Christendom": The Crusades in the *Encyclopaedia Britannica* from 1771 to 2018', in *After the Crusade: Memory and Legacy*, eds. Kurt Villads Jensen and Torben Kjersgaard Nielsen, vol. 2 (Odense, forthcoming).

52 For this approach to the reception of the crusades, see Elizabeth Siberry, 'The Crusades: Nineteenth-Century Readers' Perspectives', in *Engaging the Crusades, Volume One*, pp. 7–26.

53 See the query run at 'Pageviews Analysis: Crusades', *Wikimedia*, <https://tools.wmflabs.org/pageviews/?project=en.wikipedia.org&platform=all-access&agent=user&start=2015-07&end=2018-11&pages=Crusades>, [accessed 10 December 2018]. For different language versions of the article, see 'Langviews: Crusades', *Wikimedia*, <https://tools.wmflabs.org/langviews/?project=en.wikipedia.org&platform=all-access&agent=user&start=2015-07-01&end=2018-11-30&sort=views&direction=1&view=list&page=Crusades>, [accessed 10 December 2018].
54 For a broader comparison of crusade-related articles, see 'Pageviews Analysis: Various Articles', *Wikimedia*, <https://tools.wmflabs.org/pageviews/?project=en.wikipedia.org&platform=all-access&agent=user&start=2015-07&end=2018-11&pages=Crusades|First_Crusade|Third_Crusade|Saladin|Richard_I_of_England|Fourth_Crusade|Second_Crusade|Children%27s_Crusade|Templars|Military_Orders>, [accessed 10 December 2018].
55 'Knightfall', *imdb.com*, <https://web.archive.org/web/20181213112833/https://www.imdb.com/title/tt4555364/>, [accessed 13 December 2018].
56 König, 'Wikipedia', p. 171.
57 Skottki, 'Structural Amnesia', pp. 118–19; Tyerman, *Debate*, p. 233. See references to the work of Steven Runciman in 'Crusades', *Wikipedia*.
58 Dan O'Sullivan, 'What Is an Encyclopedia? From Pliny to Wikipedia', in *CPOV*, p. 47.
59 Ford and Geiger, 'Writing Up'; Ford and Wajcman, 'Gender Gap'.
60 Kildall and Stern, 'Wikipedia Art', p. 171.

Bibliography

Primary

alexa.com. www.alexa.com/topsites. [Accessed 3 December 2018].
'Category:Crusades'. *Wikipedia*. https://en.wikipedia.org/wiki/Category:Crusades. [Accessed 30 November 2018].
'Crusades'. *Wikipedia*. 30 November 2018. https://en.wikipedia.org/wiki/Crusades. [Accessed 30 November 2018].
'Crusades: en.wikipedia.org'. *xTools*. https://xtools.wmflabs.org/articleinfo/en.wikipedia.org/Crusades. [Accessed 7 December 2018].
'Knightfall'. *Imdb.com*. https://web.archive.org/web/20181213112833/https://www.imdb.com/title/tt4555364/. [Accessed 13 December 2018].
'Langviews: Crusades'. *Wikimedia*. https://tools.wmflabs.org/langviews/?project=en.wikipedia.org&platform=all-access&agent=user&start=2015-07-01&end=2018-11-30&sort=views&direction=1&view=list&page=Crusades. [Accessed 10 December 2018].
'Pageviews Analysis: Crusades'. *Wikimedia*. https://tools.wmflabs.org/pageviews/?project=en.wikipedia.org&platform=all-access&agent=user&start=2015-07&end=2018-11&pages=Crusades. [Accessed 10 December 2018].
'Pageviews Analysis: Various Articles'. *Wikimedia*. https://tools.wmflabs.org/pageviews/?project=en.wikipedia.org&platform=all-access&agent=user&start=2015-07&end=2018-11&pages=Crusades|First_Crusade|Third_

126   *Mike Horswell*

Crusade|Saladin|Richard_I_of_England|Fourth_Crusade|Second_
Crusade|Children%27s_Crusade|Templars|Military_Orders. [Accessed 10
December 2018].
'Portal:Crusades'. *Wikipedia.* https://en.wikipedia.org/wiki/Portal:Crusades.
[Accessed 30 November 2018].
similarweb.com. https://web.archive.org/web/20181203102832/https://www.
similarweb.com/top-websites. [Accessed 3 December 2018].
'Talk:Crusades/Archive 1'. *Wikipedia.* https://en.wikipedia.org/wiki/Talk:
Crusades/Archive_1. [Accessed 4 December 2018].
'Talk:Crusades/Archive3'. *Wikipedia.* https://en.wikipedia.org/wiki/Talk:
Crusades/Archive_3. [Accessed 4 December 2018].
'Talk:Crusades/Archive4'. *Wikipedia.* https://en.wikipedia.org/wiki/Talk:
Crusades/Archive_4. [Accessed 4 December 2018].
'Talk:Crusades/Archive5'. *Wikipedia.* https://en.wikipedia.org/wiki/Talk:
Crusades/Archive_5. [Accessed 5 December 2018].
'Talk:Crusades/Archive8'. *Wikipedia.* https://en.wikipedia.org/wiki/Talk:
Crusades/Archive_8. [Accessed 5 December 2018].
'Talk:Crusades/Archive9'. *Wikipedia.* https://en.wikipedia.org/wiki/Talk:
Crusades/Archive_9. [Accessed 5 December 2018].
'The Moz Top 500'. *moz.com.* https://web.archive.org/web/20181203110705/
https://moz.com/top500. [Accessed 3 December 2018].
Wiegand, Friedrich. 'Crusades'. In *The New Schaff-Herzog Encyclopedia of
Religious Knowledge*, ed. Samuel Macauley Jackson. New York: Funk &
Wagnalls Company, 1909.
'Wikipedia:Crusades'. *Wikipedia.* 30 November 2018. https://web.archive.org/
web/20181130164144/https://en.wikipedia.org/wiki/Crusades. [Accessed 30
November 2018].
'Wikipedia:Neutral point of view'. *Wikipedia.* https://en.wikipedia.org/wiki/
Wikipedia:Neutral_point_of_view. [Accessed 10 December 2018].
'Wikipedia:Notability'. *Wikipedia.* https://en.wikipedia.org/wiki/Wikipedia:
Notability. [Accessed 10 December 2018].
'Wikipedia:Ten things you may not know about Wikipedia'. *Wikipedia.*
https://en.wikipedia.org/wiki/Wikipedia:Ten_things_you_may_not_
know_about_Wikipedia. [Accessed 12 December 2018].

Secondary

Asbridge, Thomas. *The Crusades: The War for the Holy Land.* London:
Pocket Books, 2010.
Burke, Peter. *A Social History of Knowledge II: From the Encyclopédie to
Wikipedia.* Cambridge: Polity, 2012.
Chazan, Robert. *European Jewry and the First Crusade.* Los Angeles: Univer-
sity of California Press, 1996.
Christiansen, Eric. *The Northern Crusades.* 2nd edn. London: Penguin Books,
1997.
Cohen, Noam. 'Conspiracy Videos? Fake News? Enter Wikipedia, the "Good
Cop" of the Internet'. *Washington Post Online.* 6 April 2018. https://web.

archive.org/web/20180614045810/https://www.washingtonpost.com/out-look/conspiracy-videos-fake-news-enter-wikipedia-the-good-cop-of-the-internet/2018/04/06/ad1f018a-3835-11e8-8fd2-49fe3c675a89_story. html?utm_term=.1e1ce25a2d95. [Accessed 3 December 2018].

Cohn, Norman. *The Pursuit of the Millennium: Revolutionary Millenarians and Mystical Anarchists of the Middle Ages.* Rev. edn. New York: OUP, 1970.

Crawford, Paul. 'The First Crusade: Unprovoked Offense or Overdue Defense?'. In *Seven Myths of the Crusades.* eds. Alfred J. Andrea and Andrew Holt. Indianapolis, IN: Hackett, 2015, pp. 1–28.

Davies, Norman. *Europe: A History.* London: Pimlico, 1997.

Ellenblum, Ronnie. *Crusader Castles and Modern Histories.* Cambridge: CUP, 2007.

Fallis, Don. 'Toward an Epistemology of Wikipedia'. *Journal of the American Society for Information Science and Technology* 59:10 (2008), pp. 1662–74.

Ford, Heather. 'Fact Factories: Wikipedia and the Power to Represent'. PhD Thesis. University of Oxford, 2015.

———. 'Foreword: Wikipedia and the Sum of All Human Knowledge'. *Nordisk Tidsskrift for Informationsvidenskab Og Kulturformidling* 5:1 (2016), pp. 9–14.

Ford, Heather and R. Stuart Geiger. '"Writing Up Rather than Writing Down": Becoming Wikipedia Literate'. In *Proceedings of the Eighth Annual International Symposium on Wikis and Open Collaboration.* Linz: ACM, 2012, pp. 1–4.

Ford, Heather and Judy Wajcman. '"Anyone Can Edit", Not Everyone Does: Wikipedia's Infrastructure and the Gender Gap'. *Social Studies of Science* 47:4 (2017), pp. 511–27.

Fullerton, Lindsay and James Ettema. 'Ways of Worldmaking in Wikipedia: Reality, Legitimacy and Collaborative Knowledge Making'. *Media, Culture & Society* 36:2 (2014), pp. 183–99.

Haverinen, Anna. 'Internet Ethnography: The Past, the Present and the Future', *Ethnologia Fennica* 42 (2015), pp. 79–90.

Horswell, Mike. 'From "Superstitious Veneration" to "War to Defend Christendom": The Crusades in the *Encyclopaedia Britannica* from 1771 to 2018'. In *After the Crusade: Memory and Legacy.* eds. Kurt Villads Jensen and Torben Kjersgaard Nielsen. Vol. 2. Odense: University Press of Southern Denmark, forthcoming.

———. *The Rise and Fall of British Crusader Medievalism, c.1825–1945.* Abingdon: Routledge, 2018.

Kedar, Benjamin Z., et al. 'The Crusading Kingdom of Jerusalem – The First European Colonial Society? A Symposium'. In *The Horns of Hattin*, ed. Benjamin Z. Kedar. London: Variorum, 1987, pp. 341–66.

Kildall, Scott and Nathaniel Stern. 'Wikipedia Art: Citation as Performative Act'. In *CPOV*, pp. 165–90.

Knight, Charles and Sam Pryke. 'Wikipedia and the University, A Case Study'. *Teaching in Higher Education* 17:6 (2012), pp. 649–59.

König, René. 'Wikipedia'. *Information, Communication & Society* 16:2 (2013), pp. 160–77.

Lock, Peter. *The Routledge Companion to the Crusades.* Abingdon: Routledge, 2006.

Lovink, Geert and Nathaniel Tkacz. 'The "C" in CPOV: Introduction to the CPOV Reader'. In *CPOV*, pp. 9–13.

Mesgari, Mostafa, Chitu Okoli, Mohamad Mehdi, Finn Årup Nielsen, and Arto Lanamäki. '"The Sum of All Human Knowledge": A Systematic Review of Scholarly Research on the Content of Wikipedia'. *Journal of the Association for Information Science and Technology* 66:22 (2015), pp. 219–45.

O'Sullivan, Dan. 'What Is an Encyclopedia? From Pliny to Wikipedia'. In *CPOV*, pp. 34–49.

Phillips, Jonathan. *Holy Warriors: A Modern History of the Crusades.* London: Vintage, 2009.

———. *The Fourth Crusade and Sack of Constantinople.* London: Pimlico, 2005.

Prawer, Joshua. *The Crusaders' Kingdom: European Colonialism in the Middle Ages.* Rev. edn. London: Phoenix Press, 2001.

Queller, Donald E. and Thomas F. Madden. *The Fourth Crusade: The Conquest of Constantinople.* 2nd edn. Philadelphia: University of Pennsylvania Press, 1999.

Reagle, Joseph. 'The Argument Engine'. In *CPOV*, pp. 14–33.

Riley-Smith, Jonathan. *The Crusades: A History.* 3rd edn. London: Bloomsbury, 2014.

———. *What Were the Crusades?* 4th edn. Basingstoke: Palgrave Macmillan, 2009.

Rubenstein, Jay. *Armies of Heaven: The First Crusade and the Quest for Apocalypse.* New York: Basic Books, 2011.

Siberry, Elizabeth. 'The Crusades: Nineteenth-Century Readers' Perspectives'. In *Perceptions of the Crusades from the Nineteenth to the Twenty-First Century: Engaging the Crusades, Volume One*, eds. Mike Horswell and Jonathan Phillips. Abingdon: Routledge, 2018, pp. 7–26.

Skågeby, Jörgen. 'Online Ethnographic Methods: Towards a Qualitative Understanding of Virtual Community Practices'. In *Handbook of Research on Methods and Techniques for Studying Virtual Communities: Paradigms and Phenomena*, eds. Ben Kei Daniel. Hershey, PA: IGI Global, 2011, pp. 410–28.

Skottki, Kristin. 'The Dead, the Revived and the Recreated Pasts: "Structural Amnesia" in Representations of Crusade History'. In *Perceptions of the Crusades from the Nineteenth to the Twenty-First Century: Engaging the Crusades, Volume One*, eds. Mike Horswell and Jonathan Phillips. Abingdon: Routledge, 2018, pp. 79–106.

Tyerman, Christopher. *God's War: A New History of the Crusades.* London: Penguin, 2007.

———. *The Debate on the Crusades.* Manchester: MUP, 2011.

———. *The Invention of the Crusades.* New York: Palgrave Macmillan, 1998.

8 Engaging the crusades in context

Reflections on the ethics of historical work

Susanna A. Throop

It is a common cliché to imagine academia as an ivory tower, segregated from the rest of society, preoccupied with its own distinct concerns. Yet, academics and non-academics alike are equally fascinated with the crusades in the early twenty-first century. Most obviously, the crusades remain present in national and global politics. On the one hand, white supremacists in the U.S.A. and Europe identify with crusaders. Protesters in the 2017 Unite the Right rally in Charlottesville, Virginia, carried Deus Vult crosses.[1] Roughly a year later, German activists at an AfD demonstration in Rostock waved a Templar flag.[2] On the other hand, Islamist groups such as IS and al-Qaeda also use the idea of ongoing Western crusading to motivate their followers.[3] Additionally, the crusades remain widespread in general pop culture. The video game *Crusaders of Light* launched in spring 2018, joining popular favourites such as *Assassin's Creed*, *Crusader Kings* and *Stronghold: Crusader.* In December 2017, the TV series *Knightfall* premiered on the History Channel; it was renewed in August 2018.[4] Memes using the crusades continue to proliferate and be highly popular; for example, two Reddit forums, r/CrusadeMemes and r/DankCrusadeMemes, have over 17,000 and 14,000 subscribers, respectively.[5] Teachers and scholars, too, are focused on the crusades, reflecting the ubiquity of the crusades in political discourse and pop culture. School teachers, journalists and academics have come together in various combinations to discuss the study, teaching and modern invocation of the crusades.[6] Of course, countless scholarly publications on the medieval crusades also continue to stream forth.

Clearly, academic discourse on the crusades is occurring in the context of political discourse on and popular fascination with the crusades. But it is also occurring in at least two other contexts. First, medieval studies as a wider field is engaged in conversations about the connection of our work and white supremacist movements. Second, the function, purpose and implementation of higher education in the U.S.A. and the U.K. are under scrutiny. What does 'public engagement' mean and how can it be assessed? What is the relationship between higher education, job preparation and good citizenship? How does scholarly expertise contribute to society, and how can those contributions – whether inside or outside the classroom – be measured?

In this brief personal essay, I reflect in broad terms on these conversations for those who study the history of the crusades narrowly and without reference to the contexts outlined above; consequently, the overview I provide here may seem insufficient to those involved in the conversations I reference.[7] Ultimately, I suggest, high levels of public and scholarly engagement with the crusades and the multiple contexts in which this engagement is taking place should lead us to consider and act upon the ethical dimension of our work as scholars, teachers and writers of history. I make this argument from my own subject position to reinforce the broader point that we necessarily work within subjective and contextual positions.

Intimately entangled: the past, history and historical expertise

The high volume of political and popular discourse on the crusades corresponds to the widespread use of a remembered Middle Ages (i.e., the Middle Ages as imagined-to-have-been) to justify discrimination or violence in the twenty-first century. Admittedly, the remembered Middle Ages have long played a key role in political and popular cultures.[8] In particular, the remembered Middle Ages has been and continues to be used to buttress key elements of modern identities, particularly nationality, gender (especially masculinity), religion and/or race.[9]

Within the remembered Middle Ages, the crusades are most frequently invoked as a 'poster conflict of civilizational clash'.[10] That is, the history of the crusades seems to offer a historical example of a world broken into separate, homogenous and mutually antagonistic societies, a world in which modern identity categories were present, aligned and demarcated – those of one race and religion lived here, those of another lived there. Additionally, in this world, masculine hierarchies of power seem to have been firmly in place; men ruled and took action, including the waging of war, whilst women remained passively at home. The remembered Middle Ages with their crusades thus seem to stand in opposition to a multicultural and feminist modernity.[11] Depending on perspective, then, the remembered Middle Ages can function as a sign of an escaped dark age that should be fully buried, or a lost golden age that should be actively revived.

These remembered Middle Ages are the product, rather than a distortion, of scholarly work. It is deeply difficult to disentangle the study of the medieval past and the study of medievalisms, i.e., representations or memories of the medieval past.[12] Medieval studies as a field emerged in the nineteenth century and itself constituted a medievalism; early medievalists created their own remembered Middle Ages.[13] Historians of crusading have long recognised that historiography is essential for understanding the crusades[14]; I would add that this is because the modern term 'crusade', and the various and contradictory concepts it communicates depending on context and audience, represents an interpretation of the past, rather than the past itself. We have to discuss the historiography of the crusades because, arguably, the phenomenon does not fully exist outside a historiographical framework.

Thus, the remembered Middle Ages (with remembered crusades) that are so influential in the early twenty-first century have their roots in the work of medievalists over the past two centuries. In other words, crusader medievalisms in popular discourse are not new nor have they arisen separate from the academic study of the past; rather, as many have noted, they reflect past scholars' construction of medieval history and the history of the crusades.[15] Certainly, new work is repeatedly illuminating the intimate relationship between 'scholarly' and 'popular' histories of the crusades; for example, at the International Medieval Congress at Leeds in July 2018, multiple papers illustrated the connections between the history of the crusades, nation-building and Western imperialism.[16]

Yet, it is not only the historical ideas of earlier generations of scholars that continue to exert influence but also their gendered and racialised conceptualisations of expertise and authority. Ironically, our scholarly spaces continue to reflect the imagined hegemony and homogeneity of medieval Europe as asserted by previous centuries of scholars.[17] Scholarly expertise is still frequently expected to reflect gender, race and class hierarchies, and not all scholarly spaces are welcoming to those who do not fit the unwritten standards for expertise. As a result, the identities of those who acquire and exercise expertise at the highest levels remain largely homogenous and normative. Statistically speaking, the higher one moves up the scale within academia – from graduate student or contingent instructor at one end to tenured full professor at the other – the more normative one is likely to be in terms of race, gender, sexuality and virtually every other category.[18]

These dynamics are magnified in the public realm and directly intersect with ongoing debates about academic labour, public engagement and the function of higher education. At the same time, that calls for public engagement increase, the dynamics of online public engagement may also reinforce normative hierarchies of expertise. Whilst the explosion of publishing options and platforms like Twitter allows for the diversification of scholarly voices and scholarly modes of engagement, in practice the institutional structures of academic labour and hierarchy and the performances of expertise and authority that are most recognised serve to underscore a narrowly defined academic elite. Even though everyone is theoretically subject to harassment online, those scholars who engage the public online with the least risk and most reward are those whose identities conform to normative expectations of expertise in terms of age, gender, race and class. Those who are thought not to resemble an expert or professional scholar, including younger academics, women and scholars of colour, are more likely to encounter mass abuse and threatened violence.[19]

In addition, the way that academic expertise is typically performed in both popular and scholarly realms – namely, by publicly addressing large groups of people, either in spoken or written word, by claiming to possess 'the facts', and by skill in debating and 'defeating' intellectual opponents – also compound the problem. Even when undertaken online, these performances of expertise still conform to those established in the creation and institutionalisation of the discipline of history in the nineteenth and early twentieth centuries.[20] The dynamics of scholarly engagement with the public in a mass media world, then, have the potential to enhance and reinforce the privileged hegemony of historical expertise within the academy, creating a vicious cycle that is hard (though not impossible) to disrupt. To put it as bluntly as possible, those scholars who are most likely to be rewarded and least likely to be abused for engaging the public are those who, whether intentionally or not, affirm the idea that expertise exists in certain kinds of bodies and manifests in certain kinds of scholarly performance. The more controversial or 'relevant' a historical topic is – for example, the crusades – the more these dynamics may be exaggerated.

Whilst medieval studies as a field is increasingly discussing its own diversity and inclusion, the field of crusade studies is not yet engaged in the kind of similar conversations that are taking place in other areas of medieval studies.[21] There are many possible explanations for this absent conversation; however, if the reason is that scholars of crusade studies do not value diversity or are unconcerned with inclusion in their field, then that, too, is a point of connection between academia and 'extremists' on various sides who also are unconcerned with, if not openly hostile towards, diversity and inclusion. Moreover, if we write books and give lectures that confirm a normative model of historical expertise and a heterosexual, masculinist, white and Christian history of the crusades, we reinforce political and popular discourses that centre the same vision of the crusades in their calls for violent action. And when on social media we meet historical assertions that we consider false with bald counter-claims of expertise – claims of dominance based on identity rather than evidence – we may ironically perpetuate the same normative model of expert knowledge that is recognised by those who critique evidence-based arguments.

In sum, then, the remembered crusades and remembered Middle Ages encountered in twenty-first–century political and popular discourses are a modern refashioning of older ideas created by scholars. Whilst it may be appealing to categorise the ubiquity of the crusades in modern political and popular discourses as the result of 'co-option', 'appropriation' or 'misuse', ultimately the way the crusades are utilised in public discourse results from, and mirrors, academia in terms of scholarly ideas, scholarly hierarchies and scholarly performances of expertise. And the way that expertise on the crusades is often performed and embodied in both public and scholarly spaces likewise echoes the exclusionary politics of disciplinary power put in place in the nineteenth century and still largely maintained. Our work as scholars is intimately entangled with the very same popular and political discourses that we may protest; we are inextricably enmeshed in our socio-historical contexts.

Working intentionally

The way we represent the crusades in our scholarship and teaching, and the identities and performances of expertise we choose to recognise and elevate, have significant ramifications for our field, higher education and the world in which we all live. The points of connection I've outlined above should lead us to ask: when we study and write and teach the crusades, 'whose work are we doing and why?'[22] We have choices to make about how we do our work, and we should make them intentionally. Above all, I encourage us to undertake self-reflection, to actively consider both the ethics and the limits of history, to engage the public in the complexity of history, and to acknowledge the interconnections between the teaching and writing of history and its public understanding.

First, as scholars of the crusades, we can and should engage in critical self-reflection. We already recognise that engaging with the historiography of the crusades is a necessary first step for studying the crusades; let us go one step further and ask, what are 'the crusades' that we construct through our writing and teaching? Are they a singular phenomenon that epitomises the medieval world and affirms the idea of the Middle Ages as an era of unmitigated 'civilisational conflict', or are they one of many intersecting and at times contradictory phenomena? Are they another category of war, an exercise in cultural domination, or an exalted form of spiritual exercise? (Can they be all or none of these?) Why do we choose to distinguish 'the crusades' as an analytical category distinct from other Christian religious wars? Whose perspectives do we prioritise if we make such a distinction, and whose perspectives do we lose? In raising these questions, I am not suggesting a return to the debates on the definition of crusading that occupied prior generations of historians, but rather, following Kristin Skottki, pushing us towards a more critical self-awareness based on an understanding of the role we play in constructing the history of the crusades.[23]

To dig even deeper, why are so many of us so interested in the crusades? What drives our study of these and not other wars? Does the term 'crusade' allow us to distance ourselves from what was suffering and death for past people? [24] Who are we – what privileged subject positions might we occupy – if we discuss the crusades with personal detachment? When we distinguish the crusades from other forms of warfare and Christian violence – when we accept that there was something that distinguished crusading violence from other violence – we may inevitably prioritise the perspective of those who supported crusading and viewed it as superior to other forms of violence, rather than the perspectives of those who experienced crusading violence. This gives me pause.

As we reflect on our study of the crusades, we can and should consider the ethical dimensions of historical work in general. An active relationship between the way we do history and the world in which we do it is not new; major changes in the historical profession have virtually always corresponded to an 'attempt to address the political and cultural transformation of the age'.[25] Since history is used to promote a variety of political calls to action (sometimes violent), as historians and human beings, we have a pressing obligation to consider our ethical response to the uses of history and recognise our role in constructing it. As Gabrielle Spiegel asserted in 2013:

> the greatest issue facing the practice of history today is to understand its relationship to ethical goals long banished from

professional historiography. In the end, what is at stake in these discussions is not an epistemological question of "truth" but an ethical response.[26]

These points resound in the context of the history of the crusades. Those of us who study and construct this history in our writing and teaching have not only to grapple with the ethics of studying warfare and violence – acts with ethical dimensions in their own times as well as in our own – but also with the ethics of studying a past that is itself being used to promote present and future warfare and violence. As historians, of course we care about the past, i.e., 'what happened'. In our current contexts, however, the greatest challenge is how we should respond to what has happened and continues to happen, and what may happen in the future. As David Matthews expresses it, 'when someone describes his torture at the hands of a western state as "medieval," our first concern should not be historical accuracy'.[27] We have a responsibility not only to support historical accuracy and evidence-based argumentation but also to consider the present and future ethical dimensions of our words in the twenty-first–century world.

Some may raise concerns that historians' biases will distort historical knowledge. Yet working in the aftermath of the post-modern critique of empiricism, many of us already recognise that our biases *unavoidably* affect historical knowledge. We are already working with an awareness of our limitations as human beings with embodied minds and individual subject positions. Not only is 'neutrality not optional',[28] total objectivity is unattainable, and the very dream of objectivity is itself historically contingent.[29] Recognising this, we are already attempting to delineate the ethics as well as the very boundaries of our profession in an era that can perhaps be best characterised by its 'affective engagement' with the past.[30] Because the work of history has ethical connotations in the world/s in which we live, the question is not whether we *can* engage in the work of history ethically, but rather *how* we should do so. How may we best operate as professional historians who are also moral beings concerned with ethical obligations to past, present and future?

Answering this question will surely require us to recognise both the lessons of historiography and the limits of historicism. María Inés Mudrovcic notes that when facing an ethical crisis in the present, most historians' automatic reaction is to provide a narrative of how that ethical crisis came about. Such a narrative, however, creates the sense that the present is inevitable, set and unavoidable; it has the potential to legitimise continuity over time as a foundation for ethical action in the present and future.³¹ But continuity over time is no such thing. To give an obvious example, a long legacy of the racist enslavement of people in the U.S.A. does not mean that racism and racialised labour dynamics in the twenty-first century are legitimate or inevitable. The past has clearly influenced the present, but the extent and nature of that influence is not predetermined. Knowledge of the past can and should inform our view of the present and our plans for the future, but it does not decide our ethical obligations in the present, nor does it dictate a path towards an ethical future. This is particularly true when we recognise the contingent and revisionist nature of historical knowledge. We remain agents capable of ethical choices, regardless of what has happened – or is thought to have happened – in the past. As historians of the crusades, a controversial subject directly connected to past and present violence, we cannot afford to lose sight of this. Should we do so, we will perpetuate the status quo, whether we intend to or not.³²

Second, as scholars of the crusades, we can and should engage in critical and collective conversation about the state of our field. How equitable are our scholarly communities and dialogues? In a time when many are pointing yet again to the legacy of institutionalised racism and sexism in shaping and gatekeeping academic communities, some professional societies have affirmed their commitment to supporting the work and humanity of scholars from under-represented groups in academia.³³ Will crusade studies do the same? If not, what historical evidence and scholarly perspectives will we be excluding and what will be the consequences of those exclusions? After all, if we are unwilling to acknowledge and change long-standing institutional inequities in our field, that choice will affirm that the identities of those we have deemed 'expert' scholars of the crusades will match the identities of those whom white supremacists believe should wield power.

Third, awareness of the contexts in which we work as scholars of the crusades should lead us to reconsider how we engage the public. The all-too-common binary discourse of 'correct v. incorrect' history is insufficient on its own when engaging the public. It can oversimplify complex matters, obscure processes of historical production and downplay problems of interpretation. It often relies upon a claim of expertise that may be assumed to be racialised and gendered. In addition, it may seem to suggest that historical accuracy correlates with ethical action – i.e., that the primary problem with a call for violence based on the history of the crusades is epistemological rather than ethical. And lastly, it is an intellectually unsustainable approach, given the complexity of the history of the crusades.

Instead, I suggest we seek out modes of public engagement that acknowledge complexity and demonstrate (rather than simply assert or perform) expertise. Historians can still counter selective interpretations of the past by providing broader and deeper perspectives. Those perspectives should be complex both because the past was complex *and* because complexity encourages us to ask questions, consider alternatives, rethink assumptions and acknowledge complications. Those perspectives should also be complex and non-binary because the various calls for violent action based on crusade history rely upon the opposition of multiple binaries, Christianity v. Islam for example, that only partly reflect our historical sources.

In addition, we can acknowledge the connection between the writing of history, the teaching of history and public knowledge of history. These connections are many. Our choice of topics, our course design and our pedagogies often reflect the importance we accord to certain subjects, the availability of written teaching materials and the degree to which we believe students will be likely to engage with a particular topic. Given that the idea of the crusades as a story of 'civilisational conflict' is dominant and popular in our world, our sense of historical significance and relevance, the number and kind of written texts available for teaching, and perceived student engagement may all conceivably drive us to create learning experiences that further reinforce the idea of the crusades as 'civilisational conflict'. These factors, combined with the relative low prestige accorded to the writing of teaching texts, may also encourage us to affirm rather than question or complicate traditional Eurocentric and crusader-centric narratives of crusading history, in some cases simply because it will be easier to do so or because alternative teaching materials are not readily available.

There are double binds implicit in these issues, and they defy easy resolution. To the best of our knowledge, the crusades were a ubiquitous part of the cultural background of Latin Christendom through the Middle Ages and into the modern period. If we disconnect the crusades from medieval history, we run the risk of deliberately failing to acknowledge that cultural ubiquity. If we acknowledge the cultural ubiquity, we run the risk of appearing to confirm that the crusades can be seen as representative of a culturally bifurcated and civilisationally conflicted Middle Ages. One way forward is to write and teach crusading as inclusively and non-Eurocentrically as possible; another possibility is to use the ubiquity of crusading to move the focus to the broader picture of which crusading was one piece.[34] A third possibility is to offer courses that appeal to students' pre-existing belief in the centrality of the crusades as 'us v. them' civilisational conflict but that, over the span of the course, critically call that belief into question by relentlessly emphasising historical complexity and contingency.

Underlying all of these possibilities is the importance of recognising that teaching, and writing texts for teaching is meaningful public engagement and comes with its own ethical responsibilities. In 2019, it is relatively common to acknowledge that teaching via civic engagement or public digital platforms constitutes public engagement.[35] Yet, it is worth remembering that *any* teaching is public engagement, since those being taught are members of the public; indeed, the idea of higher education as an effort for the public good has historically supported – or been claimed to support – many systems of higher education worldwide. Classroom teaching is not awarded the prestige of the major public lecture or scholarly monograph, nor does it usually reach the audience of thousands theoretically available online, and too often now it is undertaken by the most contingent and least recognised as 'expert' amongst us, but it offers unparalleled opportunities for dialogue and learning. Depending on instructors' choice of pedagogies, teaching also has the potential to disrupt the normative model of expertise.[36]

If we recognise teaching as meaningful public engagement – and public engagement as a form of teaching – we are challenged not only to reconsider how we imagine 'expertise' but also to think hard about what and for whom we are writing. Furthermore, if we acknowledge that first exposure to ideas about the crusades and the Middle Ages occurs in childhood, we need to ask what we are doing to support pre-college schooling. In the U.S.A., most public school teachers are under-resourced, underpaid, and given extremely little or no time to teach pre-modern history. What can we, as academics, do to support our school teachers? How can we help make our knowledge accessible and easy to incorporate in their teaching, and how can we help ensure that students learn the habits of mind critical to the study of history, not just 'the facts', before university? Some are already partnering with school teachers to do this work, and it is time for more of us to do so.[37]

Conclusion

Those of us who study the history of the crusades and construct this history in writing are not working in isolation within an ivory tower. We are working as embodied people, enmeshed in institutional structures and social hierarchies, and alongside intense engagement with the crusades in modern political and pop cultures. The relationship between the academic study of, and public attention to, the crusades is a most intimate one, as is the relationship between hierarchies of power and performances of expertise inside and outside academia. Given these points, it is imperative that we heed Geraldine Heng's observation that 'our work can be made to assume other burdens than what we had designed'.[38] Acknowledging the contexts in which we work should be followed by both reflection and a renewed commitment to intentional ethical action, as individual scholars and as a scholarly community. We have choices to make that will affect not only our field but our societies and our world, and given the current uses of the crusades in modern discourse, those choices will almost certainly echo broadly beyond academia, whether or not we have considered their ethical dimensions in advance.

Notes

1 E.g. 'Deconstructing the Symbols and Slogans Spotted in Charlottesville', *Washington Post*, 18 August 2017, <https://www.washingtonpost.com/graphics/2017/local/charlottesville-videos/?utm_term=.47d9fdad38ef>, [accessed 13 December 2018].
2 For photographs of this protest, see '14.05.2018 – AFD-Demonstration – Rostock', *EXIF: Recherche & Analyse*, <https://exif-recherche.org/?envira=14-05-2018-afd-demonstration-rostock>, [accessed 13 December 2018].
3 See Andrew B.R. Elliott, *Medievalism, Politics and Mass Media: Appropriating the Middle Ages in the Twenty-First Century* (Woodbridge, 2017), Chs 5 and 8.
4 Joe Otterson, '"Knightfall" Renewed at History with New Showrunner, Mark Hamill Joins Cast', *Variety*, 13 August 2018, <https://variety.com/2018/tv/news/knightfall-renewed-season-2-history-mark-hamill-1202903138/>, [accessed 13 December 2018].
5 r/CrusadeMemes, Reddit, < https://www.reddit.com/r/CrusadeMemes/>, [accessed 20 February 2019]. r/dankcrusademes, Reddit, <https://www.reddit.com/r/dankcrusademes/>, [accessed 3 September 2018].
6 'Teaching History in the Age of the Alt-Right', *Teaching History in the 21st Century: Teaching History Conference*, University of California at Berkeley, 5–6 May 2017. 'The Middle Ages, the Crusades, and the Alt Right: A Symposium for Scholars and Journalists', George Washington University, 13 October 2017. Symposia include 'The Modern Appropriation of the Crusades' (Manchester, February 2018); the International Medieval Congress at the University of Leeds, July 2018, roundtable discussion 'Teaching the Crusades in an Age of White Nationalism' and multiple sessions on the 'Memory of the Crusades' and 'Engaging the Crusades.'
7 My thanks to the series and volume editors, especially Mike Horswell, for the invitation to submit such a reflective piece.
8 Ready examples of this can be seen within this series. In addition, see Marcus Bull, *Thinking Medieval: An Introduction to the Study of the Middle Ages* (Basingstoke, 2005); Bruce Holsinger, *Neomedievalism, Neoconservatism, and the War on Terror* (Chicago, 2007) and Elliott, *Medievalism*.

Connections between pop culture and the Middle Ages can be found in the latter.

9 E.g., see Katie Stevenson and Barbara Gribling, eds, *Chivalry and the Medieval Past* (Cambridge, 2016); Horswell, *British Crusader Medievalism*, pp. 66–88; and Kelly J. Baker, '"God Give Us Men!" The Klan's Christian Knighthood', in *Gospel According to the Klan. The KKK's Appeal to Protestant America, 1915–1930* (Lawrence, 2011), pp. 97–121. On the role of historical memory in modern political cultures, see María Inés Mudrovcic, 'About lost futures or the political heart of history', *Historein* 14:1 (2014), pp. 7–21, especially discussion of the work of Tsvetan Todorov, *Les abus de la mémoire* (Paris, 2004) at p. 14.

10 Umej Bhatia, *Forgetting Osama bin Munqidh, Remembering Osama bin Laden: The Crusades in Modern Muslim Memory* (Singapore, 2008), p. 65.

11 Demonstrated in Elliott, *Medievalism*.

12 For an introduction to the study of medievalisms, see David Matthews, *Medievalism: A Critical History* (Cambridge, 2015).

13 Matthews, *Medievalism*, esp. pp. ix–xii; Bull, *Thinking Medieval*, pp. 47–8.

14 Tyerman, *Debate*; Norman Housley, *Contesting the Crusades* (Malden, 2006).

15 This point is made emphatically by Kristin Skottki, 'The dead, the revived, and the recreated pasts. "Structural amnesia" in representations of crusade history', in *Engaging the Crusades*, Vol. 1, pp. 107–32. See also Heng, 'Holy War Redux'.

16 Seen particularly in papers by Simon A. John, Pedro A. G. Martins, Luigi Russo, and Elizabeth Siberry.

17 See Sara Ahmed, *On Being Included: Racism and Diversity in Institutional Life* (Durham, NC, 2012); Gabriella Gutiérrez y Muhs, Yolanda Flores Niemann, Carmen G. González, and Angela P. Harris, eds., *Presumed Incompetent: The Intersections of Race and Class for Women in Academia* (Boulder, 2012); Patricia A. Matthew, ed, *Written/Unwritten: Diversity and the Hidden Truths of Tenure* (Chapel Hill, 2016); and Remi Joseph-Salisbury, 'Whiteness Characterizes Higher Education Institutions – So Why Are We Surprised by Racism?', *The Conversation*, 9 March 2018, <http://theconversation.com/whiteness-characterises-higher-education-institutions-so-why-are-we-surprised-by-racism-93147>, [accessed 13 December 2018].

18 Martin J. Finkelstein, Valerie Martin Conley, and Jack H. Schuster, *Taking the Measure of Faculty Diversity*, TIAA Institute, April 2016, <https://www.tiaainstitute.org/publication/taking-measure-faculty-diversity>, [accessed 13 December 2018]; summarised in Colleen Flaherty, 'More Faculty Diversity, Not on Tenure Track', *Inside Higher Ed*, 22 August 2016, <https://www.insidehighered.com/news/2016/08/22/study-finds-gains-faculty-diversity-not-tenure-track>, [accessed 13 December 2018]. Hannah Atkinson et al. *Race, Ethnicity & Equality in UK History: A Report and Resource for Change*, Royal Historical Society, October 2018, <https://5hm1h4aktue2ue-jbs1hsqt31-wpengine.netdna-ssl.com/wp-content/uploads/2018/10/RHS_race_report_EMBARGO_0001_18Oct.pdf>, [accessed 13 February 2019].

19 To see efforts to resist and undermine such stereotypes, see the hashtags #ilooklikeaprofessor and #ilooklikeahistorian on social media. For an introduction to online harassment, see Maeve Duggan, 'Online Harassment

Engaging the crusades in context 141

2017', *Pew Research Center*, <http://www.pewinternet.org/2017/07/11/online-harassment-2017/>, [accessed 13 December 2018]; and 'Online Abuse 101', *Women's Media Center*, <http://www.womensmediacenter.com/speech-project/online-abuse-101>, [accessed 13 December 2018]. For discussion of 'the increasingly public consequences of academic Twitter', see Bonnie Stewart, 'In Public: The Shifting Consequences of Twitter Scholarship', *Hybrid Pedagogy*, 14 April 2015, https://hybridpedagogy.org/in-public-the-shifting-consequences-of-twitter-scholarship/, [accessed 20 February 2019].
20 Bonnie G. Smith, *The Gender of History: Men, Women, and Historical Practice* (Cambridge MA, 2000).
21 Sierra Lomuto, 'White Nationalism and the Ethics of Medieval Studies', *In the Middle*, 5 December 2016, <http://www.inthemedievalmiddle.com/2016/12/white-nationalism-and-ethics-of.html>, [accessed 13 December 2018]; Medievalists of Color, 'Statement on Race and Medieval Studies', 1 August 2017, <https://medievalistsofcolor.com/statements/on-race-and-medieval-studies/>, [accessed 13 December 2018]; Dorothy Kim, 'Teaching Medieval Studies in a Time of White Supremacy', *In the Middle*, 28 August 2017, <http://www.inthemedievalmiddle.com/2017/08/teaching-medieval-studies-in-time-of.html>, [accessed 13 December 2018]; Helen Young, 'Medievalfail', *In the Middle*, <http://www.inthemedievalmiddle.com/2017/08/medievalfail.html>, [accessed 13 December 2018]; Matthew Gabriele, 'Why the History of Medieval Studies Haunts How We Study the Past', *Forbes*, 14 July 2018, <https://www.forbes.com/sites/matthewgabriele/2018/07/14/history-medieval-studies-haunts-study-past/#23fcf99d6b52>, [accessed 13 December 2018].
22 Here I paraphrase and apply the words of Dr. Nadia Altschul at the International Medieval Congress in Leeds in 2018. In the roundtable 'Creating the Medieval Studies We Want to Remember', Altschul also called for a 'self-critical medieval studies'.
23 Skottki, "Structural Amnesia".
24 For sustained analysis of historical distance, see Mark Salber Phillips, *On Historical Distance* (New Haven, 2013).
25 María Inés Mudrovcic, 'Historical Narrative as a Moral Guide and the Present as History as an Ethical Project', *Historia da Historiografia* 21 (2016), pp. 10–24, at p. 20.
26 Gabrielle M. Spiegel, 'Above, About and Beyond the Writing of History: A Retrospective View of Hayden White's *Metahistory* on the 40th Anniversary of its Publication', *Rethinking History* 17:4 (2013), pp. 492–508, at p. 505.
27 Matthews, *Medievalism*, p. 178.
28 Kim, 'Teaching Medieval Studies'.
29 Michel-Rolph Trouillot, *Silencing the Past: Power and the Production of History*, 2nd rev. edn. (Boston, 2015); Peter Novick, *That Noble Dream: The 'Objectivity' Question and the American Historical Profession* (Cambridge, 1988).
30 Salber Phillips, *On Historical Distance*, p. 232. See also Trouillot, *Silencing the Past*, Ch. 5.
31 Inés Mudrovcic, 'Historical Narrative as a Moral Guide', pp. 21–2.
32 Kim, 'Teaching Medieval Studies'.

33 See TEAMS Featured Lesson Resource Page: Race, Racism, and the Middle Ages, under 'Recent Letters, Declarations, and Petitions', <https://teams-medieval.org/?page_id=76>, [accessed 13 December 2018].
34 Brian A. Catlos, *Infidel Kings and Unholy Warriors: Faith, Power, and Violence in the Age of Crusade and Jihad* (New York, 2014). I have attempted to do this in my most recent book, *The Crusades* (Leeds, 2018).
35 Travis Holland, 'The Public Necessity of Student Blogging', *Hybrid Pedagogy*, 13 November 2018, <https://hybridpedagogy.org/public-necessity-student-blogging/>, [accessed 15 February 2019].
36 Julie Fellmayer, 'Disruptive Pedagogy and the Practice of Freedom', *Hybrid Pedagogy*, 11 October 2018, <https://hybridpedagogy.org/disruptive-pedagogy-and-the-practice-of-freedom/>, [accessed 15 February 2019].
37 *Berkeley History-Social Science Project*, <http://ucbhssp.berkeley.edu/>, [accessed 15 February 2019].
38 Heng, 'Holy War Redux', p. 424.

Bibliography

Primary

'14.05.2018 – AFD-Demonstration – Rostock'. *EXIF: Recherche & Analyse.* https://exif-recherche.org/?envira=14-05-2018-afd-demonstration-rostock. [Accessed 13 December 2018].

Atkinson, Hannah, Suzanne Bardgett, Adam Budd, Margot Finn, Christopher Kissane, Sadiah Qureshi, Jonathan Saha, John Siblon, and Sujit Sivasundaram. *Race, Ethnicity & Equality in UK History: A Report and Resource for Change.* Royal Historical Society, October 2018. https://5hm1h4aktue2uejb-s1hsqt31-wpengine.netdna-ssl.com/wp-content/uploads/2018/10/RHS_race_report_EMBARGO_0001_18Oct.pdf. [Accessed 13 February 2019].

Berkeley History-Social Science Project. http://ucbhssp.berkeley.edu/. [Accessed 15 February 2019].

Duggan, Maeve. 'Online Harassment 2017'. *Pew Research Center.* www.pewinternet.org/2017/07/11/online-harassment-2017. [Accessed 13 December 2018].

Finkelstein, Martin J., Valerie Martin Conley, and Jack H. Schuster. *Taking the Measure of Faculty Diversity.* TIAA Institute, April 2016. www.tiaainstitute.org/publication/taking-measure-faculty-diversity. [Accessed 13 December 2018].

Medievalists of Color. 'Statement on Race and Medieval Studies'. 1 August 2017. https://medievalistsofcolor.com/statements/on-race-and-medieval-studies/. [Accessed 13 December 2018].

'Online Abuse 101'. *Women's Media Center.* www.womensmediacenter.com/speech-project/online-abuse-101. [Accessed 13 December 2018].

r/crusadememes. *Reddit.* www.reddit.com/r/crusadememes/. [Accessed 20 February 2019].

r/dankcrusadememes. *Reddit.* www.reddit.com/r/dankcrusadememes/. [Accessed 3 September 2018].

Robinson, Carol L. 'Featured Lesson Resource Page: Race, Racism, and the Middle Ages'. *Teaching Association for Medieval Studies*. https://teams-medieval.org/?page_id=76. [Accessed 13 December 2018].

Secondary

Ahmed, Sara. *On Being Included: Racism and Diversity in Institutional Life*. Durham, NC: Duke University Press, 2012.
Baker, Kelly J. *Gospel According to the Klan. The KKK's Appeal to Protestant America, 1915–1930*. Lawrence, KS: University of Kansas Press, 2011.
Bhatia, Umej. *Forgetting Osama bin Munqidh, Remembering Osama bin Laden: The Crusades in Modern Muslim Memory*. Singapore: S. Rajaratnam School of International Studies, 2008.
Bull, Marcus. *Thinking Medieval: An Introduction to the Study of the Middle Ages*. Basingstoke: Palgrave Macmillan, 2005.
Catlos, Brian A. *Infidel Kings and Unholy Warriors: Faith, Power, and Violence in the Age of Crusade and Jihad*. New York: Farrar, Straus and Giroux, 2014.
Elliott, Andrew B. R. *Medievalism, Politics and Mass Media: Appropriating the Middle Ages in the Twenty-First Century*. Woodbridge: Boydell and Brewer, 2017.
Fellmayer, Julie. 'Disruptive Pedagogy and the Practice of Freedom'. *Hybrid Pedagogy*, 11 October 2018. https://hybridpedagogy.org/disruptive-pedagogy-and-the-practice-of-freedom/. [Accessed 15 February 2019].
Flaherty, Colleen. 'More Faculty Diversity, Not on Tenure Track'. *Inside Higher Ed*, 22 August 2016. www.insidehighered.com/news/2016/08/22/study-finds-gains-faculty-diversity-not-tenure-track. [Accessed 13 December 2018].
Gabriele, Matthew. 'Why the History of Medieval Studies Haunts How We Study the Past'. *Forbes*, 14 July 2018. www.forbes.com/sites/matthewgabriele/2018/07/14/history-medieval-studies-haunts-study-past/#23fcf99d6b52. [Accessed 13 December 2018].
Gutiérrez y Muhs, Gabriella, Yolanda Flores Niemann, Carmen G. González, and Angela P. Harris, eds. *Presumed Incompetent: The Intersections of Race and Class for Women in Academia*. Boulder, CO: University Press of Colorado, 2012.
Heng, Geraldine. 'Holy War Redux: The Crusades, Futures of the Past, and Strategic Logic in the "Clash" of Civilizations'. *PMLA* 126:2 (2011), pp. 422–31.
Holland, Travis. 'The Public Necessity of Student Blogging'. *Hybrid Pedagogy*, 13 November 2018. https://hybridpedagogy.org/public-necessity-student-blogging/. [Accessed 15 February 2019].
Holsinger, Bruce. *Neomedievalism, Neoconservatism, and the War on Terror*. Chicago, IL: Prickly Paradigm Press, 2007.
Horswell, Mike. *The Rise and Fall of British Crusader Medievalism, c. 1825–1945*. Abingdon: Routledge, 2018.
Housley, Norman. *Contesting the Crusades*. Malden: Blackwell Publishing, 2006.

144　*Susanna A. Throop*

Inés Mudrovcic, María. 'About Lost Futures or the Political Heart of History'. *Historein* 14:1 (2014), pp. 7–21.

————. 'Historical Narrative as a Moral Guide and the Present as History as an Ethical Project'. *Historia da Historiografia* 21 (2016), pp. 10–24.

Joseph-Salisbury, Remi. 'Whiteness Characterizes Higher Education Institutions – So Why Are We Surprised by Racism?'. *The Conversation*, 9 March 2018. http://theconversation.com/whiteness-characterises-higher-education-institutions-so-why-are-we-surprised-by-racism-93147. [Accessed 13 December 2018].

Kim, Dorothy. 'Teaching Medieval Studies in a Time of White Supremacy'. *In the Middle*, 28 August 2017. www.inthemedievalmiddle.com/2017/08/teaching-medieval-studies-in-time-of.html. [Accessed 13 December 2018].

Lomuto, Sierra. 'White Nationalism and the Ethics of Medieval Studies'. *In the Middle*, 5 December 2016. www.inthemedievalmiddle.com/2016/12/white-nationalism-and-ethics-of.html. [Accessed 13 December 2018].

Matthew, Patricia A., ed. *Written/Unwritten: Diversity and the Hidden Truths of Tenure*. Chapel Hill, NC: University of North Carolina Press, 2016.

Matthews, David. *Medievalism: A Critical History*. Cambridge: D.S. Brewer, 2015.

Novick, Peter. *That Noble Dream: The 'Objectivity' Question and the American Historical Profession*. Cambridge: CUP, 1988.

Otterson, Joe. '"Knightfall" Renewed at History with New Showrunner, Mark Hamill Joins Cast'. *Variety*, 13 August 2018. https://variety.com/2018/tv/news/knightfall-renewed-season-2-history-mark-hamill-1202903138/. [Accessed 13 December 2018].

Phillips, Mark Salber. *On Historical Distance*. New Haven, CT: Yale University Press, 2013.

Skottki, Kristin. 'The Dead, the Revived, and the Recreated Pasts. "Structural Amnesia" in Representations of Crusade History'. In *Perceptions of the Crusades from the Nineteenth to the Twenty-First Century: Engaging the Crusades, Volume One*. eds. Mike Horswell and Jonathan Phillips. Abingdon: Routledge, 2018, pp. 107–32.

Smith, Bonnie G. *The Gender of History: Men, Women, and Historical Practice*. Cambridge, MA: Harvard University Press, 2000.

Spiegel, Gabrielle M. 'Above, About and Beyond the Writing of History: A Retrospective View of Hayden White's *Metahistory* on the 40th Anniversary of its Publication'. *Rethinking History* 17:4 (2013), pp. 492–508.

Staff. 'Deconstructing the Symbols and Slogans Spotted in Charlottesville'. *Washington Post*, 18 August 2017. www.washingtonpost.com/graphics/2017/local/charlottesville-videos/?utm_term=.47d9fdad38ef. [Accessed 13 December 2018].

Stevenson, Katie and Barbara Gribling, eds. *Chivalry and the Medieval Past*. Cambridge: D.S. Brewer, 2016.

Stewart, Bonnie. 'In Public: The Shifting Consequences of Twitter Scholarship'. *Hybrid Pedagogy*, 14 April 2015. https://hybridpedagogy.org/in-public-the-shifting-consequences-of-twitter-scholarship/. [Accessed 20 February 2019].

Throop, Susanna A. *The Crusades. An Epitome.* Leeds: Kismet Press, 2018.

Trouillot, Michel-Rolph. *Silencing the Past: Power and the Production of History.* 2nd rev. edn. Boston, MA: Beacon Press, 2015.

Tyerman, Christopher. *The Debate on the Crusades.* Manchester: MUP, 2011.

Utz, Richard. *Medievalism: A Manifesto.* Kalamazoo, MI: Arc Humanities Press, 2017.

Young, Helen. 'Medievalfail'. *In the Middle*, 31 August 2017. www.inthemedievalmiddle.com/2017/08/medievalfail.html. [Accessed 13 December 2018].

Index

For Product Safety Concerns and Information please contact our EU
representative GPSR@taylorandfrancis.com
Taylor & Francis Verlag GmbH, Kaufingerstraße 24, 80331 München, Germany

www.ingramcontent.com/pod-product-compliance
Ingram Content Group UK Ltd.
Pitfield, Milton Keynes, MK11 3LW, UK
UKHW021424080625
459435UK00011B/154